LEGAL PROBLEMS of SCHOOL BOARDS

Being Volume 5 of the

Legal Problems of Education Series

SPONSORED BY

The National Organization on Legal Problems of Education

ARTHUR A. REZNY, Ph.D.

EDITOR IN CHIEF

Associate Professor of Education, Department of Administration and Supervision, University of Wisconsin-Milwaukee; co-author of The Schoolman in the Law Library; contributor to the Law of Guidance and Counseling.

CINCINNATI

THE W. H. ANDERSON COMPANY

CONTRIBUTORS

MANNY S. BROWN
Chapter 2: Records of School Board Meetings

ARTHUR A. REZNY
Chapter 1: School Board Procedure and Non-Delegable Power

REYNOLDS C. SEITZ
Chapter 6: Public Employee Negotiating and School Board Authority

THOMAS A. SHANNON
Chapter 4: School Board Communications

AUGUST W. STEINHILBER
Chapter 5: De Facto Segregation

MARLIN M. VOLZ
Chapter 3: Remedies Against School Boards and School Board Members as to Records and Procedures

FOREWORD

This book attempts to explore legal principles pertaining to some of the involvements of a school board in current issues on the educational scene. An attempt is made to do more than review litigation. It is hoped the reader will discover sound guide lines for the better operation of our public schools in a nation dedicated to the principles of a democratic philosophy. The public school, as one of the educational agencies in a community and acting as an agent of the state, is responsible for aiding in the fulfillment of this complex American dream.

The National Organization on Legal Problems of Education (NOLPE) was organized by a group of persons especially interested in the area of school law. Membership is open to all interested individuals. At present the membership includes: attorneys-at-law who are counsels for school districts, professors of law, professors of education with a specialty in school law, school administrators, and other professional individuals.

This book is the fifth in a series of books on legal problems of education to be prepared and published through the sponsorship of NOLPE. Other publications of the organization are: *Law and the School Superintendent, Law and the School Principal, An Evaluation of Existing Forms of School Laws,* and *Law of Guidance and Counseling.*

The contributors to this volume are highly qualified individuals who gave freely of their knowledge and time. Whatever royalties are realized from this publication are placed in the treasury of NOLPE. It is in this manner the organization is capable of carrying out other activities to further the study and research in the field of school law for a better society.

Arthur A. Rezny
Editor in Chief

TABLE of CONTENTS

Chapter 1: SCHOOL BOARD PROCEDURE AND NON-DELEGABLE POWER

Chapter 2: RECORDS OF SCHOOL BOARD MEETINGS

Chapter 3: REMEDIES AGAINST SCHOOL BOARDS AND SCHOOL BOARD MEMBERS AS TO RECORDS AND PROCEDURES

INTRODUCTION

The major purpose of this book is to bring forth the relationship of the operation of the school board with present day problems. One of the major problems in writing a book on *Legal Problems of School Boards* is to develop some continuity.

School boards have not been faced with dynamic educational problems for many years, probably not since the Kalamazoo case in 1874, when it was held by the great jurist, Judge J. Cooley of the Michigan Supreme Court, that it was within the authority of the school board to establish and maintain high schools in the absence of express legislative authority. However, school boards have been confronted with profound issues related to an exploding school population and the growth and the complexity of our society.

We are faced with keeping our citizenry informed. We are faced with a society, pluralistic in nature, that has the responsibility to contribute to a better society. There is a tendency by many to fail to identify themselves as a part of this great society and to wish to attain an identity that may or may not foster an improved society for all. The current issues are the perennial separation of church and state, de facto segregation, and collective bargaining. In the midst of these issues is the board of education of the public schools.

It is with the above in mind that this book was conceived; it is concerned with two of the current issues—mainly—de facto segregation and collective bargaining as related to the operation of the school board from a legal base and from a procedural concept—communications. To lend continuity, the basis for school board procedure, with emphasis on nondelegable powers, is presented in Chapter 1. The necessity for keeping the house in good order is established in Chapter 2, "Records of School Board Meetings." It naturally follows that any violation of the establishment of good record keeping is subject to examination. In Chapter 3, "Remedies Against School Boards and School Board Members as to Records and Procedures," a series of involvements is presented. The purpose is more than a review of what has been but should enable attorneys, school board members, and administrators to carefully examine procedures in current and future issues brought before the school board.

The background developed in Chapters 1, 2, and 3 leads into the three chapters covering current problems. Chapter 4, "School Board Communications," is a subject that has not been presented in any other document in the detail of issues, procedures, and suggested practices. This chapter covers the complexities of external and internal communications. The emphasis is on keeping the citizenry and staff informed, and on the great issue of the relationship of communications to morale in the community and the school system. What greater problem faces our public schools today?

The importance of school board communications is directly related to Chapters 5 and 6. Chapter 5, "De Facto Segregation," clearly reviews the litigation, raises the many questions involved in the issue, and presents some solutions. The reader may wish to ask himself whether some of the procedures discussed in previous chapters would have alleviated the tensions developed in the community regarding de facto segregation.

Chapter 6, "Public Employee Negotiating and School Board Authority," is presented from both a philosophical and factual point of view. Without a review of the legal involvements and procedures that must be followed, no school board can reach an intelligent understanding of this issue. The willingness to communicate properly may well be the key to a better understanding of this issue.

It seems mandatory for the reader to relate each chapter with the other. There is a flow, there is continuity, there is review, and above all else there is provocation of thought. The outcome should be the better operation of school boards, the development of outstanding members of school boards, and the development of improved administration of the public schools in the United States.

Chapter 1

SCHOOL BOARD PROCEDURE AND NON-DELEGABLE POWER

by

ARTHUR A. REZNY

Associate Professor of Education, Department of Administration and Supervision, University of Wisconsin-Milwaukee; co-author of The Schoolman in the Law Library; contributor to the Law of Guidance and Counseling and to educational journals; formerly associated with the public schools in the states of Michigan and Illinois as an administrator and classroom teacher.

Chapter 1

SCHOOL BOARD PROCEDURE AND NON-DELEGABLE POWER

Section

§ 1.1 Introduction

The trend toward larger school districts may complicate the operation of school boards. The increase in the size of the school district has lead to a reduction in the number of school districts in the United States. However, much litigation still continues. West's, *General Digest, Third Series,* 1964, records over 500 entries under the heading "Schools and School Districts." Many of these cases involve the operation of the local school board.

The purpose of this chapter is to look at the operation of the school board. With the change suggested above, there seems to be a trend to include lay groups in the decision-making process and, because of the complexity of the many problems of society, to the establishment of ad hoc committees of the board of education to investigate and report findings. Because of this trend, the emphasis will be to look at litigation relative to non-delegable powers, rather than to review all of the issues in the operation of a school board.

Chapter 2 discusses school board records and Chapter 3 discusses remedies against school board members.[1]

§ 1.2 In general

School district business can be legally transacted at a legal meeting of the school board. The litigation always concerns the charge that business was transacted at an illegal board meeting or that a board exceeded its discretionary power. The statutes, in general, provide for direction regarding regular meetings.

Special meetings or call meetings present a different problem. Where state statutes make specific requirements as to method or nature of notification, these are, of course, controlling. In the absence of such provision, courts have generally agreed that the method of notification is immaterial so long as actual notice is given to each member, by one possessing the authority to call a meeting or issue the order to call a meeting, a reasonable time prior to the time set for the meeting. What constitutes a "reasonable time" can only be determined by the circumstances of each particular situation. It must at least be contemplated, however, that under the conditions ordinarily prevailing, notice will reach each member in sufficient time to permit him to arrange to attend the meeting. The exceptions to this rule are governed by extenuating circumstances. By its very name the purpose of a special meeting is to consider or act on some particular matter prior to the time of the next regular session. It is, therefore, important that the notice of a special meeting state with particularity and clarity the purpose of the meeting, i.e., the matters to be considered, as well as the time and place of meeting.

---

[1] See: Robert R. Hamilton and E. Edmund Reutter, Jr., Legal Aspects of School Board Operation. New York: Bureau of Publications, Teachers College, Columbia University, 1958; see also Robert L. Drury and Kenneth C. Ray, Principles of School Law. New York: Appleton-Century-Crofts, 1965.

Whether a meeting is considered regular or special, such meetings are public meetings. In some jurisdictions, the statutes provide for closed sessions or executive sessions when certain items of business are considered, such as the discussion of personnel or the purchasing of a school site.

In general, a quorum is a simple majority unless the statutes mandate a specific number of board members. Each board member has a right to vote. Abstaining from voting does not indicate a negative vote and even though the majority vote on an issue is less than a majority of the quorum, the courts have upheld the legality of the vote.

The school board is empowered to adopt rules, regulations, and procedures. Such adoptions must be considered reasonable acts. Although it is difficult to adopt rules and regulations for every situation, it is much easier to adopt procedures for action. The courts have held consistently that a school board may not violate its own procedures. The lack of adopting a set of procedures for various administrative tasks may lead to a poorly administered school system. Since the emphasis in this treatise is upon current issues that involve the community and professional staff, the need for sound procedures seems quite evident.

§ 1.3 Non-delegable powers—board committees

A school board must clearly understand the difference between the exercise of judgment and discretion and the performance of administrative or ministerial duties. The courts have held quite consistently that the board of education cannot delegate its powers unless they are of administrative or ministerial nature.

The leading case dates back to 1907 in Iowa. The school board decided to construct a new school building, and delegated a committee of the board of education to carry out its wishes. The committee selected a site, adopted plans for construction, and awarded contracts. Action was brought to enjoin the school board from carrying out the contract. The Supreme Court of Iowa upheld the illegality of the contracts when it said:

> May the board delegate to a committee the power to select and procure title to a building spot, to advertise for bids for the erection of a schoolhouse, to act as a building committee and to see to the erection and completion of the building?
> While it is a general rule that power conferred upon a public board or body cannot be delegated, yet a public corporation or municipality or instrumentality of government may, like a private corporation or persons, do its ministerial work by agents or committees . . . . Where the act to be done involves judgment or discretion, it cannot be delegated to any agent or committee.[2]

This basic principle of law still prevails and the authority of this case still holds, since it is cited as late as 1962 in a case involving another type of governmental agency, as distinguished from a board of education.[3]

In North Carolina a school board appointed a property committee to sell school land. The contract was attacked on the grounds that such power could not be delegated to a committee of the board of education. The Supreme Court of North Carolina followed the same principle of law as the court of Iowa when it said:

> It is also alleged and admitted that before the contract was made with Harrison, the defendants' board of trustees, by a resolution, delegated the entire matter of the sale of the property to a committee of four, with the sole limitation that the price should not be less than $3,500, and declared that the action of the committee should be final. This is an allegation and admission that the trustees attempted to delegate a non-

---

[2] Kinney v. Howard, 133 Iowa 94, 110 NW 282 (1907).
[3] State v. Johnston, 253 Iowa 674, 113 NW(2d) 309 (1962).

delegable power and responsibility. It means that they attempted to abdicate their solemn trust by a delegation of their authority. "The principle is a plain one, that the public powers or trusts devolved by law or charter upon the council or governing body, to be exercised by it when and in such manner as it shall deem best, cannot be delegated to others. This principle may not prevent the delegation of duties which are ministerial, but where the trust committed to the governing body involves the exercise of functions which partake of a judicial character, it may not be delegated."[4]

In Pennsylvania a school board became involved in the disbursement of extracurricular funds. Although this case, in main, revolves around the issue of whether extracurricular funds are public school funds, the board of education appointed a special committee to the athletic board with full power of control. The court was as decisive as the courts of Iowa and North Carolina when it said:

> Statutes do not authorize the members of a school board to appoint certain of its members as an athletic board of control and to delegate to them full control over extracurricular activities, including the right to receive and expend fees for admission to athletic events. . . . The board of athletic control must be considered merely as a committee, with like powers and duties as a teachers' committee, the committee on supplies, or the building committee.[5]

§ 1.4 —Board members

In North Carolina the board of education delegated the power to employ a principal to individual members of the board. The court simply held:

---

[4] Bowles v. Fayetteville Graded School, 211 NC 36, 188 SE 615 (1936).

[5] In re German Township School Directors, 46 D&C 562 (Pa, 1942).

> Where a power is intrusted to a board, such as a county board of education, composed of different individuals, the board can exercise such power only in a regular or special meeting attended by at least a quorum of its members. It cannot perform its functions through its members acting individually, informally, and separately.[6]

§ 1.5 —Joint boards

There may be a tendency to look upon cooperative action by two boards as a worthy procedure. Such cooperation can come through the joint action of two boards of education. Also, with the advent of intermediate school districts and cooperative regional agencies, each school board must look carefully at its procedures.

In California a high school district and an elementary school district deemed it advisable to employ the same principal. Although the statutes permitted certain kinds of action as a joint board, the court held that the employment of a principal was a power that could not be delegated when it said:

> As upon the question of organization as a joint board, the high school board could not delegate to the elementary board the power to employ or to participate in the employment of a principal of the high school, but the law contemplates that each board must determine for itself, in the manner provided for the determination of other questions, whether or not it will agree to the employment of the same person as principal of both schools and who such person will be.[7]

---

[6] Iredell County Board of Education v. Dickson, 235 NC 358, 70 SE(2d) 14 (1952).

[7] Cloverdale Union High School Dist. v. Peters, 88 CalApp 731, 264 Pac 273 (1928).

The above cases point out clearly that the board of education cannot delegate its powers to committees of the board of education, to individuals of the board of education, or, unless provided by the law, to action by a joint board. The courts in consistently sustaining this position have been as consistent in upholding that the board may delegate administrative or ministerial duties.[8]

Boards of education will have to continue to appraise their practices.

§ 1.6 Non-board committees—in general

"In no sense is any citizens group intended to replace the legally constituted school board or even to compete with it in the eyes of the community."[9] This statement by Edward Mowbray Tuttle, First Executive Secretary of the National School Boards Association, Inc., seems so axiomatic that it seems surprising that a school board could become involved in any litigation. It also seems axiomatic that there should be an understanding by the public that cooperation on the community level may mean the involvement of citizen groups in the decision-making process. Tuttle emphasized this point when he said:

> That a clear understanding shall exist from the start that, while the citizen committees are free to carry on their work in the manner which seems to them best, there shall be a close working relationship with the established school authorities, and that the recommendations of the committees shall be channeled through the board of education for final approval and action.[10]

It is only recently the courts have been confronted with this trend. The courts have been faced with the direct ques-

---

[8] Eddy v. Omaha, 72 Neb 550, 103 NW 692 (1905).

[9] Edward Mowbray Tuttle, School Board Leadership in America, Danville, Illinois: The Interstate Printers and Publishers, 1963, p. 134.

[10] Id., p. 133.

tion of the use of an official advisory committee, the use of an informal advisory committee, and the use of a state legislative investigating committee.

§ 1.7 —Formal advisory

In 1964, action was brought against the board of education of the city of Chicago. One of the many allegations in this case was against the use of any advisory committee by the mayor of the city of Chicago for the nomination of school board members for approval by the city council. This committee was composed of heads of universities, civic, business, labor and professional organizations who served at the mayor's request. The allegation insisted that the legislature never intended to empower private individuals with this authority. The statute is quite clear that the legislature empowered the mayor to submit appointments for the board of education to the city council for approval. The advisory committee submitted to the mayor a list for his consideration. The allegation further contended that the advisory committee adopted criteria for nominees in addition to the statutory qualifications for appointment set forth in the statute. The allegation stated that by the use of the advisory committee the mayor "bound himself," particularly by his statements made during an election campaign, that he would follow the advice of the committee. The Supreme Court of Illinois looked very carefully at the function of an advisory committee and it stated:

> That serious consideration of count V is unmerited is apparent. No action by the mayor could bind the members of the city council, whose approval is required by section 34-3. The mayor has not, by seeking the advice and suggestions of the advisory commission, legally restricted his appointees to those individuals thus recommended. If such pre-election statements of intention were made, they would not prevent his subsequent action to the contrary, if his judgment so dictates. As

> the trial court aptly stated in referring to the relationship between the mayor and the commission, "consultation is not abdication."[11]

The use of any advisory committee then falls into the category of consultative rather than authoritative in the decision-making process.

§ 1.8 —Informal advisory

The use of a most informal advisory committee is noted in a rather recent case in New York. At a special meeting of the school district the taxpayers voted down the purchase of a school site. The school board was concerned about this defeat and called a non-public meeting and invited interested citizens to participate in the discussion to put up the proposition for the purchase of a school site for a new vote. Although the emphasis of this decision rests on a public meeting, the relationship of a board of education and a group of citizens is commented upon when the court stated:

> Next it is alleged that the board met in a special meeting to which they invited a "number of representative citizens" to join them, and together they unanimously agreed in this closed session to put the proposition up for a new vote. Such a proceeding is highly irregular and must be condemned. All official action must be taken at a public meeting, and not at a closed one which only certain members of the public are permitted to attend.[12]

It should be noted that official action was taken at this closed meeting. If the reasoning of the Illinois court were to be followed, it could be concluded that the board of education could have sought the advice of this special commit-

[11] Latham v. Board of Education, 31 Ill(2d) 178, 201 NE(2d) 211 (1964).

[12] Application of Flinn, 154 NYS(2d) 124 (1956).

tee of citizens and, at a later official meeting, called for official action.

§ 1.9 —Other agencies

A procedural question was raised in the state of Florida on the use of a state legislative committee. The teaching certificates of teachers were revoked by the state board of education on the basis of the investigation of an investigator representing a committee of the Florida state legislature. The certificates were revoked on the grounds of homosexuality. The issue in the case was on procedures and the relationship of a state legislative investigating committee and the state board of education. The state board of education was empowered to revoke a certificate or license. The investigator was an employee of the state legislative investigating committee. The state legislative investigating committee was to investigate subversive activities. The state superintendent of public instruction, who was a member of the state board of education, agreed with the chairman of the state investigating committee to have the investigator seek evidence about activities of teachers. The Supreme Court of Florida was faced with the issue of the statutory provisions for such an investigation, and the relationship of the legislative committee and the state board of education. The court clarified this relationship when it stated:

> It would have been a relatively simple matter for the state agency to have followed Section 229.08 (16). Instead of doing so the basic requirement of a preliminary investigation to determine probable cause was completely ignored. In lieu of following the statute, the state board relied upon a so-called investigation by an investigator (Strickland) for the State Legislative Investigations Committee. This man had not been appointed by the state board. He claims to have proceeded solely for the legislative committee, but, as aforestated, in accord with some understanding between the com-

mittee chairman and the state superintendent to the effect that any evidence of sexual perversion in the public schools would be reported to the state superintendent.[13]

Although the above case is on the state level, the importance of this case to the use of committees on the local level is quite apparent. Procedures established by statutes must be followed. The responsibility cannot be delegated to another state agency. Likewise, the local school board is empowered to establish reasonable procedures for sundry items. Any violations of procedures established on the local level will not be upheld by the courts.

The recency of the above cases seems to indicate a trend towards litigation in the area of committees. The courts have upheld the principle that the board of education cannot delegate its powers. In view of the problems confronting school boards today and the advisability of using lay committees to aid in the solution of problems, the board of education should carefully outline the procedures for the use of advisory committees. If nothing else, it will avoid public embarrassment over issues.

§ 1.10 Conclusion

The school board is an administrative unit of government. It is an agent of the state and is given mandatory, directory, or permissive powers to carry out the educational program established by the state. The board of education carries out these tasks in legally held school board meetings. Such meetings, whether regular or special, must abide by the statutes. Litigation involves business transacted at an illegal board meeting or when a board acts unreasonably in the interpretation of its discretionary power. The school board must be legally organized and carry on its business in a prudent manner. The board of education, except by stat-

[13] Neal v. Bryant (Fla), 149 S(2d) 529 (1962).

utory provision, cannot delegate its authority to committees of the board, to individuals of the board, to a joint board, to a citizen advisory committee, whether formal or informal, or to other governmental agencies. The school board may delegate its ministerial duties to others.

Chapter 2

RECORDS OF SCHOOL BOARD MEETINGS

by

MANNY S. BROWN

Member of the Wisconsin Bar; school board member, Racine, Unified School District No. 1, Racine, Wisconsin; State Assemblyman, Racine Second District, State of Wisconsin; and author.

Chapter 2

RECORDS OF SCHOOL BOARD MEETINGS

§ 2.1 Introduction

The local school district is a creature of the legislature. The school board of the local school district acts as an agent of the state. The state by mandatory, permissive, and directory legislation directs the operation of the school board. Within this broad power, the state mandates the school board to conduct its business in an orderly manner. The records of school board meetings aid in the fulfillment of this process.

§ 2.2 Recording of the minutes

In order for meetings of school boards to be valid, certain statutory requirements must be met. These statutes vary from state to state but generally are of the same substance and clarity. In most jurisdictions, a board of school directors is expressly required to keep minutes or a record of its proceedings.

The courts have said that school boards "can only act through their minutes,"[1] and that a board speaks only through its minutes and many problems and difficulties in-

[1] Cheatham v. Smith, 229 Miss 803, 92 S(2d) 203 (1957).

volving school boards and third parties can be avoided through the keeping of complete and accurate minutes.[2]

There is no doubt that board records are the only legal evidence of what was done during a board meeting.[3] Paramount reasons why such records should be kept are these, according to the Illinois Supreme Court:

> Proper minutes and records should be kept by a board of education, to the end that the persons who are carrying the tax load may make reference thereto and that future boards may be advised of the manner of disposition of questions that have arisen.[4]

Therefore, we can conclude that the recording of school board minutes must be said to be mandatory according to the directives of state statutes, such as Wisconsin Statute, sec. 40.28, Laws of 1961: "The clerk shall record the minutes of board meetings, and in his absence the board may select another member to act as clerk for the meeting.[5]"

Yet, in other jurisdictions, statutes have been held directory rather than mandatory. A Missouri court held that statutes requiring that the clerk of a school district procure necessary record books and keep a correct record of the proceedings of all meetings of the board, that contracts of employment must be recorded by and filed with the district clerk, and that duplicate copies of contracts entered into by or on behalf of the district shall be executed, and one copy filed with the clerk, were directory and not mandatory, where the clerk did not perform exactly according to the manner prescribed in the statute, because the minutes were not transcribed in the official book of the district.[6]

---

[2] Lone Jack Graded School Dist. v. Hendrickson, 304 Ky 317, 200 SW(2d) 736.

[3] Lewis v. Board of Education (Ky), 348 SW(2d) 921 (1961).

[4] Hankenson v. Board of Education, 10 IllApp(2d) 79, 134 NE(2d) 356 (1956).

[5] WisStats, sec. 40.28, Laws of 1961.

[6] Tate v. School Dist., 324 Mo 477, 23 SW(2d) 1013, 70 ALR 771.

However, courts generally have held that a school board speaks only through its minutes,[7] will use the minutes to determine the intent of the board, and normally will not admit verbal evidence to contradict a written record.[8]

The Missouri Supreme Court once said: "the record is not only the best evidence, but primarily is the *only* evidence by which the action of the board may be shown.[9]"

Under a statute requiring the record of a vote of school directors to show the "ayes" and "nays," a statement that that vote was unanimous is not sufficient, but yet if the record shows that all members of the board were present, and that all voted in the affirmative, the "ayes" and "nays" need not be shown more specifically.[10]

It appears, therefore, that there is unanimity of opinion that for the benefit of the community, the citizenry and public purpose, a written record must be kept of properly constituted meetings of a board of education. The form of the minutes, their sufficiency as such, may be subject to change in certain jurisdictions, but it is only through the modicum of the duly kept minutes that the citizens and their instrument, the courts, can be apprised as to what their school board is doing.

§ 2.3 Approval and attestation of minutes

As a matter of accepted school board practice, minutes of the previous meeting or meetings of the board are approved by the said board at each statutory or regular meeting of the board. Such procedure is usually the first order of business, after roll call, on the board meeting agenda. The chairman asks for additions or corrections to such minutes before a motion for approval is considered. Upon the min-

[7] Cheatham v. Smith, 229 Miss 803, 92 S(2d) 203 (1957).

[8] State ex rel School Dist. v. Smith, 336 Mo 703, 80 SW(2d) 858 (1935).

[9] Hankenson v. Board of Education, 10 IllApp(2d) 79, 134 NE(2d) 356 (1956).

[10] 12 ALR 236, 237.

utes being duly approved by a simple majority of those board members present, there being a quorum at the time, the minutes are then prepared for publication in the local newspaper, if said publication is a requirement of the law in the said jurisdiction.

Since meetings of boards of education are generally open to the public, the minutes of such meetings are a public record and are generally published in their entirety after being passed upon by the board. Indiana requires that school board minutes be signed by all members present at the meeting for which minutes were taken. Wisconsin requires that only the president and clerk, or secretary as the case might be, sign the said minutes, marking the same an official recorded document.

Board secretaries usually record the minutes after the meeting has adjourned, upon the basis of notes the said secretary has taken during the meeting. The Oklahoma Supreme Court held that this was an accepted practice and a recommended one to follow.[11] The memoranda made by a board secretary have been held by the Utah court not to be public documents. There, on the day following a school board meeting, certain citizens requested permission to examine the minutes of the meeting, and the secretary had not yet made up the minutes from his notes. Permission was therefore refused, and the court backed up the board's decision. The court said, in *Conover* v. *Board of Education:*

> The clerk's untranscribed notes reasonably are not classifiable as a public writing . . . whereas the transcribed minutes in final form, but awaiting only approval and placement in the journal, are a public writing.[12]

It appears that the Utah court made a wise decision in the *Conover* case. It would have been a dangerous prece-

[11] Gillen v. School Dist., 41 Okla 12, 136 Pac 1086, 50 LRA(NS) 99 (1913).

[12] 1 Utah(2d) 375, 267 P(2d) 768 (1954).

dent for the court to hold otherwise, because mere notes not approved by the board as minutes would have given rise to all kinds of interpretation as to what was the official record, if people could inspect such notes before transcription. Most school board meetings being open to the public, it remains only that the public take advantage of the open access generally guaranteed to that public by the statutes of the state involved.

§ 2.4 Amendments to the minutes

If minutes are discovered to be in error, such error may be corrected by amendment at the next subsequent meeting of the board following the meeting during which time the error had occurred. Common practice lists such amendment in the manner of a complete relisting of the subject under consideration as amended, with incorporation by reference to the previous minutes for which such amendment is intended.

Minutes can be amended, usually, to speak the truth of what happened at the meeting in question, but may not be amended to reflect a change in mind, for such an action might prejudice third parties who may have acted in reliance upon the minutes.

The New Hampshire Supreme Court said in *Sawyer* v. *Manchester-Keene R. Co.*:

> To permit the record to be altered or amended in accordance with facts found on the testimony of witnesses, after individuals gave . . . invested their money, or performed labor upon the faith of the votes recorded, would produce the same mischief as if no record were required. No one could safely engage in transactions with a town or with its special agents, without first ascertaining the accuracy of the record. In attempting

to do this, the same difficulty would be met as if there were no record.[13]

According to accepted Rules of Order, if there is a change in mind, there follows a motion for reconsideration of a question passed upon. To make a change in the minutes on a peremptory pique or a change of mind would be a dangerous practice board members must avoid.

Actually, there is no set rule that minutes need be amended at the very next meeting of the board following the meeting where the problem might have arisen. It is recommended that boards follow that policy, however, in order to keep a current thought as to procedure and practice. As long as the rights of third parties are not affected, as much as two years can elapse before minutes are amended. The Illinois Supreme Court held that, "The right of legislative or collective bodies to amend their records does not depend upon statute, but it is a right common to such bodies generally." The court, in the same case, further said, "It is not permissible to change the record to show that certain action was taken when in fact such action was not taken."[14]

Further evidence that the courts generally upheld the sanctity of the truth of the minutes is seen in an Ohio case where a school superintendent was discharged by a board in a meeting at which no minutes were kept. Twelve days later the clerk of the board, aided by another board member, attempted to create minutes of the meeting. The court declared the action of the board which discharged the superintendent to be of no effect, due to insufficient records, there being no official minutes of a duly constituted board meeting. [15]

---

[13] 62 NH 135 (1882).

[14] People ex rel Stewart v. Chicago, M. and St. P. R. Co., 326 Ill 179, 157 NE 200 (1927).

[15] Schafer v. Board of Education, 58 OhioLAbs 554, 94 NE(2d) 112 (1950).

§ 2.5 Omissions in the minutes

Courts have always been lenient with regard to form and word usage in the application of the law to school board minutes, when such are the subject of litigation. In that sense, the Supreme Court of Mississippi has said:

> The minutes of boards . . . will be looked upon with indulgence. Although they may be unskillfully drawn, if by a fair and reasonable interpretation their meaning can be ascertained, they will be sufficient to answer the requirements of law. [16]

And the Supreme Court of Nebraska has said:

> The records and proceedings of school district meetings are not to be given a narrow and technical construction, but should be construed in such a manner as to give effect to the manifest intention of the voters, if the same can be ascertained from the record.[17]

Minutes must be taken, however, in an accurate and careful way. Failure to keep proper minutes can often result in litigation and hardship to many, and could cost a needless waste of dollars to a community.

The conclusive quality of the written record in court is best seen in a Michigan case. There the administrator of an architect's estate tried to collect fees claimed to be due the architect on a school building project, which was to cost approximately $500,000. The board said the architect was to receive a percentage of a smaller amount, and had adopted a resolution approving and accepting the plans for the entire project, but later testified in court that this had been done "with reservations."

The court held that the minutes were conclusive on the

[16] Noxubee Co. v. Long, 141 Miss 72, 106 So 83 (1925).

[17] Quisenberry v. School Dist., 75 Neb 47, 105 NW 982 (1905).

subject and the architect was entitled to his percentage of cost. The court said:

> The minutes . . . showing the plans were approved, cannot be impugned by any mental reservations anyone had. The resolution speaks for itself. The board speaks only through its minutes and resolutions. Their import cannot be altered or supplemented by parol testimony.[18]

Generally, parol evidence can be admissible only to supply omissions in the records or to clarify a point that had been made.

§ 2.6 Authorized recording and contents

It is the duty of the secretary, in most cases, to keep the minutes of the board meetings. Such secretary may delegate to an assistant the actual taking of memoranda during a board meeting, but the minutes remain his responsibility or that of the clerk, depending on what kind of school district board is involved.

Generally, business to be covered in minutes should include names of all those present, including those who come late, with arrival noted, actions upon all communications to the board, reports of all standing and special committees and action taken thereon, business manager's report, including therein a financial statement of the general account, building fund, sinking fund, monthly vouchers, bids, purchases, the superintendent's report, including therein personnel changes, those employees hired and discharged or retiring, curriculum changes or suggestions, changes in policy to be discussed, future meeting sites and dates.

When policy is to be changed, minutes should include a copy of the old and new policy, complete salary schedules when adopted, names of all visitors giving presentations,

---

[18] Tavener v. Elk Rapids Ind. School Dist., 341 Mich 244, 67 NW(2d) 136 (1954).

and recording of board action of every resolution, including recording by name the number of ayes and nays. Most boards require roll call vote for expenditure of money.

The only times minutes of a board of education have been involved in litigation are instances when a particular subject had been omitted from the minutes, such as contracts, rules of discipline and conduct, rules relating to school entrance. These instances have happened when there has been no state statute to cover the problem.

In the above instance, it appears the courts have held that rules relating to policies set by the board need not be included in the minutes; yet, where the board has taken an action which requires a change in expenditure or employment, such action is required to be so listed in the minutes.

§ 2.7 Inspection by the public

Meetings of boards of education are open to the public everywhere, with certain notable exceptions, such as in Wisconsin, where meetings can be executive sessions if the subject content covers property matters or personnel.

Since the meetings are open to the public, it follows that the records of such meetings are public and open for inspection, unless the contents are of matters about which executive sessions were held.

Apparently, the courts hold that the right to inspect these records is one that cannot be denied, no matter in what manner the inspection is done. The Illinois court recently held that taxpayers had the right to photograph a school's financial records.

The board had refused permission to the group on the ground that while the taxpayers had the right to "examine and inspect the records with the naked eye" and also might "copy by hand these public records," they had no right to photograph the records. The court, however, held that there exists at common law the right to reproduce, copy and photograph public records as an incident to the common-law right to inspect and use public records. The court added that, "good public policy requires liberality in the right to examine public records."[19]

§ 2.8 Conclusion

It is interesting to note, in conclusion, that the school code of the state is the chief source to which one can look for the answer to a problem arising from the minutes of a board of education meeting. Generally, such code should spell out what such minutes must include. Where the code is silent, custom and practice or the particular board furnishes the answer. The guide-lines cited in this chapter may help focus the problems that may arise and suggest methods for dealing with such problems.

Records that are carefully kept can promote sound school administration, even if the law does not require that board minutes be kept as an official record.

It must also be remembered that the substance of the minutes are of more importance than the form in which they are kept, since the minutes are without a doubt the best evidence available as to action the board has taken, and have been held to be so by the Missouri Supreme Court which once said:

> Where the law requires a record of the proceedings of a board to be kept, the record is not only the best evidence but, primarily, is the only evidence by which the action of the board may be shown.[20]

---

[19] People ex rel Gibson v. Peller, 34 IllApp(2d) 372, 181 NE(2d) 376 (1962).

[20] State v. Smith, 336 Mo 703, 80 SW(2d) 858 (1935).

Chapter 3

REMEDIES AGAINST SCHOOL BOARDS AND SCHOOL BOARD MEMBERS AS TO RECORDS AND PROCEDURES

by

MARLIN M. VOLZ

Professor of Law, University of Louisville Law School; formerly Dean and Professor of Law, University of Kansas City Law School; past president, National Organization on Legal Problems of Education (NOLPE); author of West's Federal Practice Manual; co-author of Wisconsin Practice Methods (1st edition), Caldwell's Kentucky Practice and Procedure Forms; contributing author to Law and the School Principal, Law and the School Superintendent, and Law of Guidance and Counseling and author of numerous other publications in the field of law.

Chapter 3

REMEDIES AGAINST SCHOOL BOARDS AND SCHOOL BOARD MEMBERS AS TO RECORDS AND PROCEDURES

§ 3.1 Introduction

Earlier chapters in this volume describe the procedures which are to be followed by members of school boards in conducting their meetings and affairs, and in maintaining minutes of meetings and other records. This chapter is confined to a discussion of the various remedies provided by the law against school boards and school board members who fail to follow such procedures. Among such remedies, are actions for money damages, to remove a board member from office (quo warranto), to require him to act (mandamus), and to enjoin him from acting (injunction). Suggestions will also be offered as to how, in certain situations, defaults, omissions, and unintentional mistakes in procedures may be corrected without the incurrence of legal liability. Mr. Justice Holmes' reminder "that the machinery of government would not work if it were not allowed a little play in its joints"[1] applies particularly to the conduct of school board members, especially since many of their actions are of a discretionary nature.[2]

Nevertheless, school board members, as holders of positions of public trust, must conduct themselves with the circumspection appropriate to their important offices. Liability may arise from either action or non-action. Generally, such action or non-action is disclosed in the records of their meetings.[3]

School districts are creatures of state law. The duties, election, qualifications, term, and other pertinent attributes of the office of a school board member are normally set out in the statutes of each state. Often they will provide the consequences of improper action, a procedure for his removal from office, a method for filling vacancies, a description of instances when he may be held liable, etc. The beginning place in researching any legal question pertaining to the school board member must be the state statutes.

---

[1] Bain Peanut Co. v. Pinson, 282 US 499, 501, 51 SCt 228, 229, 75 LEd 482 (1930).

[2] See Lamb v. Danville School Board, 102 NH 569 (1960), 162 A(2d) 614, wherein the court stated: "It has been the consistent practice of the courts of this state to construe liberally votes at town and school meetings without regard to technicalities or the strict rules of parliamentary procedure . . . Since it does not appear that the procedure adopted by the school district violated any statutory duty, but at most was a violation of parliamentary procedure, there is no basis for holding that the resulting vote was void or illegal."

[3] Under the Illinois School Code, according to Hankenson v. Board of Education, 10 IllApp(2d) 79, 134 NE(2d) 356 (1956), "A record is required to be kept of the essential steps in the exercise by the board of its powers; every essential proceeding in the course of its exercise of its powers must appear in some written and permanent form in the records of the body authorized to act upon them; and where public officials are required to keep a record of their proceedings such record constitutes the only lawful evidence of action taken, and cannot be contradicted, added to, or supplemented by parol, assuming the record correctly states the facts as to what occurred, and subject to the board's limited power (not applicable in the case at bar) in a proper case and under proper circumstances to amend its record to make it correctly state the facts as they occurred."

§ 3.2 The decision in question

Where an aggrieved party seeks legal redress against one or more members of a school board for an erroneous action taken by it, one of the first questions is to ascertain the exact decision or action involved. Precisely what was it that the board did decide? As a general rule no official business may be transacted by the board except at a regular or special meeting. All official acts are to be recorded in the minutes of the meetings. A search of the official records of the meetings of the board must be undertaken to ascertain the action taken by the board, whether such action was final, or only an intermediate step in the process of arriving at a final decision. Under board policies, may the board be requested to reconsider the matter? Do its minutes fully and accurately disclose its action? If not, should the board be asked to amend or correct its minutes? In many instances a judicial remedy will be based on the decision of the board as disclosed in its official records.[4]

The condition of the record is therefore of the utmost importance, especially since it is generally presumed that acts of a public officer are regular and done with full authority.[5] Under the law of a particular state, a statute requiring a public body to keep an official record of its proceedings may be considered to be directory only.[6] Unless the presumption can be overcome by resort to outside evidence or by compelling the completion or correction of the record, any action against the school board or its members must fail.[7]

---

[4] This is particularly true where a review of board action is sought under an administrative review act. See Hankenson v. Board of Education, 10 IllApp(2d) 79, 134 NE(2d) 356 (1956); State v. McPhee, 6 Wis(2d) 190, 94 NW(2d) 711 (1959).

[5] 31 C.J.S. Evidence sec. 146, pages 798, 799.

[6] School District of Soldier Tp. v. Moeller, 247 Iowa 239, 73 NW(2d) 43 (1955).

[7] Ibid, in which the court stated: "The rule which we have previously stated, that the actions of a board are not void because no record is made in the official minutes but may be shown by outside evidence,

Not all actions of a board are appropriate for judicial review or consideration. A recommendation by a committee of the board is not an official act or decision of the board.[8] A letter written by a principal or superintendent reciting an action taken is not in itself an act or decision of the board.[9]

§ 3.3 Money damage suits

A review of court decisions, holding school board members liable in money damages for failure to maintain proper records or to follow correct procedures, may be helpful. Generally such liability does not extend to discretionary actions within the scope of their authority. A distinction must be made between such actions and acts of a ministerial nature, as to which liability may be incurred for wrongful conduct.[10]

---

is a salutary one. The officers and directors of small districts, such as the one involved here, are citizens who serve without compensation, whose other affairs occupy most of their time, and who are generally not trained in keeping exact records of their actions in managing the affairs of their schools. It would be an unduly harsh rule, leading to endless litigation and unjust results, to hold that no action may be upheld unless it is meticulously recorded in the official minute book."

The same lenient attitude toward the quality of the minutes of school board meetings was expressed in Linden School Dist. No. 24 v. Porter (ND), 130 NW(2d) 76 (1964), in which the Supreme Court of North Dakota observed: "In passing on the sufficiency of the minutes kept by a school board of a common school district, consideration should be given to the fact that ordinarily the members of such a board and its clerk are not experts in the field of keeping records of proceedings and that the meetings of such boards are to a large extent conducted informally. Such minutes will therefore not be given a technical construction and irregularities and informalities will be disregarded, where the minutes are sufficient to show the board's intention."

[8] Ibid.

[9] Ibid.

[10] The rules governing liability of board members are well summarized in Lipman v. Brisbane Elementary School Dist., 55 Cal(2d) 244, 359 P(2d) 465 (1961), in which one of such rules was stated to be: "While . . . a governmental agent is personally liable for torts which he commits when acting in a ministerial capacity, a different situation exists with respect to discretionary conduct. Because of important policy considerations, the rule has become established that government officials are not personally liable for their discretionary acts within the scope of their authority even though it is alleged that their conduct was malicious . . .

In *Stokes* v. *Newell,*[11] the board of trustees of the school district failed to give plaintiff a contract or to note her employment as principal of a junior high school in its minutes. In overruling a demurrer and permitting the plaintiff to maintain her action, the court observed:

> Had the appellee (plaintiff) applied seasonably for mandamus to compel an entry of the contract on the minutes of the school board, and to compel them to receive her as a teacher in the schools, she could have secured an enforcement of her contract, but her failure to do this did not absolve the board from their duty to enter the contract upon the minutes, if it was made as alleged in the declaration. Having failed to do this, the trustees breached their duty to the plaintiff, appellee here, and became liable for such damages as flowed from such breach of duty to her . . .[12]

In *Moore* v. *Babb,*[13] an action for money damages was brought against members of the board of education for salary lost by reason of their refusal to assign plaintiff a place to teach. She was found under the Kentucky Teachers' Tenure Act to have a "continuing" contract which could not be terminated except as provided in such Act. The court held that "she was entitled to continue teaching and could maintain this action for damages unless one or

---

the subjection of officials, the innocent as well as the guilty, to the burden of a trial and to the danger of its outcome would impair their zeal in the performance of their functions, and it is better to leave the injury unredressed than to subject honest officials to the constant dread of retaliation."

[11] 174 Miss 629, 165 So 542 (1936).

[12] The court went on to say: "Of course, there may be causes sufficient to justify the discharging of a teacher, but the trustees have no arbitrary authority to unlawfully terminate the contract of a teacher. It is true that officers are not liable for the honest exercise of discretionary powers confided to them, but when they go outside their powers and commit wrongs under the color of office, there is liability. They are not given immunity from willful wrongs or malicious acts."

[13] (Ky), 343 SW(2d) 373 (1960).

more of the affirmative defenses should be sustained." It remanded the case for consideration of such defenses. On the question of the liability of school board members as individuals, it stated:

> The members of a county board of education who deprive a teacher of a contract to which she has acquired the right under the terms of the statutes may be held personally liable in damages for the teacher's loss of salary in the absence of estoppel or other bar and upon proper proof. The basis of personal liability is the failure to perform a ministerial duty, and the board is exempt from liability where it has paid another teacher placed in the position.

In *Johnson* v. *Sabine Parish School Bd.*,[14] school board members were held not liable under a contract made by one of the members with a driver of the school bus, where they had not ratified it and had, in fact, employed another driver. It was reasoned that the selection of a bus driver was a discretionary act which could not be delegated to a single member of the board. Acts of a ministerial nature may be delegated.[15]

In *Lipman* v. *Brisbane Elementary School Dist.*,[16] school trustees were held liable to a school superintendent for money damages in making defamatory statements about him to newspaper reporters and the public. Such statements were found not to involve discretionary acts.

Members of school boards can be held individually liable for salaries that should have been paid to teachers who were recommended for employment by the superintendent,

---

[14] 19 LaApp 270, 140 So 87 (1932).

[15] See Looney v. Consolidated Indep. School Dist., 201 Iowa 436, 205 NW 328 (1925), holding that delivering a warrant in payment and accepting a deed to a school site were ministerial acts and not the exercise of wrongfully delegated power.

[16] 55 Cal(2d) 224, 359 P(2d) 465 (1961).

but wrongfully refused employment,[17] or who held a continuing contract and were denied a right to teach.[18] It has been recently held in Kentucky that where the board members act in good faith and in reliance upon an attorney general's opinion, a fund set aside to cover any damages which may accrue is to be used first to cover plaintiff's claim before the individual board members must stand the loss.[19]

Board members faced with a similar problem may well consider following the above procedure. Another method for avoiding possible liability, if the board deems it proper, is to correct and make amends for the earlier action where possible. In *Abrahams* v. *Board of Education,*[20] the court defined the power of a school board to correct an order, as follows:

> . . . nonjudicial officers or bodies may correct an order resulting from illegality, irregularity in vital matters or fraud. They may not act arbitrarily, nor may they revoke their determinations, nor review their orders once properly and finally made, however much they may have erred in judgment of the facts, even though injustice is the result. A mere change of mind is insufficient. Further action must, where power is not entirely spent, be for cause, with good reasons and proper motives for the correction of improper action.

In *Powers* v. *Spinner,*[21] a school board voted to rescind a salary increase to teachers, which it had earlier granted. The court sustained a demurrer to an action brought by the teachers against the individual board members. It stated:

---

17 Cottingham v. Steward, 283 Ky 615, 142 SW(2d) 171 (1940); Smith v. Beverly, 314 Ky 651, 236 SW(2d) 914 (1951).

18 Cooksey v. Board of Education (Ky), 316 SW(2d) 70 (1958).

19 Babb v. Moore (Ky), 374 SW(2d) 516 (1964).

20 209 NY(2d) 661 (1960). The court in this case permitted the board to rescind the appointment of a supervisor who had not yet entered upon her duties and who was lower on the eligible list than the person added thereto.

21 (Mass), 202 NE(2d) 246 (1964).

> The town, rather than the school committee or its individual members, would be liable for duly earned teachers' salaries which have been finally established by the school committee by a vote not rescinded. . . We need not now consider what power the school committee possesses to rescind previously voted salary increases.

Action taken outside of a board meeting, which presumably could impose personal liability upon the individual board members so acting, may be validated by subsequent ratification of the board at a duly called meeting, if the action is one which the board had power to take in the first instance.[22]

In *McCoy* v. *Louisiana State Board of Education,*[23] it was suggested that an action might lie against the individual members of a board of education for acting unconstitutionally in denying admission to Negroes.

§ 3.4 Compelling the school board to act (mandamus)

Mandamus is an appropriate remedy to compel the performance of a ministerial duty by a school board member where, being charged with the duty, he has refused to perform it. There are a number of limitations upon the use of the action of mandamus which should be noted. First, it does not lie where the right is doubtful, or where there is another adequate remedy.[24] Administrative remedies must first be exhausted.[25] It cannot be used to compel the per-

---

[22] In Linden School Dist. No. 24 v. Porter (ND), 130 NW(2d) 76 (1964), a contract by two board members acting individually outside of a board meeting was later ratified by proper board action recorded in the minutes. The court reaffirmed an earlier holding that "the minutes which ratified the contract did not need to embody the terms of the contract," such as its duration.

[23] 229 FSupp 735 (EDLa, 1964).

[24] State ex rel Phillip v. Public School Retirement System, 364 Mo 395, 262 SW(2d) 569 (en banc, 1953).

[25] State ex rel Scott v. Scearce (MoApp), 303 SW(2d) 175 (1957).

formance of an unlawful act,[26] or to compel him to decide a discretionary matter, to perform a discretionary act, or to instruct him how a matter should be decided.[27] Issuance of the writ of mandamus is largely discretionary with the court in each particular case.[28] The following cases indicate typical situations in which the action of mandamus may be used against school boards and school board members:[29]

In *Stokes* v. *Newell*,[30] the court stated that mandamus lay to compel an entry of plaintiff's contract of employment on the minutes of the school board.

Lingle v. *Slifer*[31] involved an action of mandamus by a teacher to compel her reinstatement. The court permitted the amendment of the record of the school board[32] to show that her dismissal resulted from a reorganization in which her job was abolished. Her petition for mandamus was dismissed.

In *Fleming* v. *Board of Trustees*,[33] a teacher also brought mandamus to compel her reinstatement. At a meeting of the board it was decided by a majority of the board not to reemploy her for the following year. No minutes of the meeting were kept and no formal motion or vote was recorded. Along with the clerk, one board member signed

---

[26] State ex rel Phillip v. Public School Retirement System, 364 Mo 395, 262 SW(2d) 569 (en banc, 1953).

[27] State v. Bilyeu (MoApp), 346 SW(2d) 221 (1961).

[28] State v. Tinsley, 236 SW(2d) 24, 241 MoApp 690 (1951).

[29] A member of a school board may in a proper case use mandamus against the superintendent, as in Wagner v. Redmond (La), 127 S(2d) 275 (1960), where the superintendent was compelled to furnish the board member with the names and addresses of pupils enrolled at certain schools.

[30] 174 Miss 629, 165 So 542 (1936).

[31] 8 IllApp 489, 131 NE(2d) 822 (1956).

[32] On the power to amend the court stated: "The record of a school board may be amended at any time to show what was in fact done at such proceeding . . . The Board of Education may order the clerk to amend the record of a previous meeting to show the facts, although the personnel of the board has changed and a long period of time has elapsed."

[33] 112 CalApp 225, 296 Pac 925 (1931).

the notice of dismissal served upon the plaintiff. The court decided against the plaintiff, finding from the evidence that a majority of the board expressed themselves at the meeting against her reemployment. The decision stressed that:

> There is no statutory provision of law requiring the meetings of school boards to be held at any specific time or place. There is no provision requiring the board to formally decide school board matters by a vote of aye or nay. There is no provision requiring the minutes of its proceedings to be recorded.

A parent in New York was successful in an action in the nature of mandamus to compel school officers to permit him to inspect the school records of his son.[34] A parent was held to have a common right of inspection which had not been abridged by constitution, statute, or regulation. In Louisiana a member of a school board was permitted to mandamus the superintendent of parish schools to furnish him with the names and addresses of pupils enrolled in certain schools.[35] In *State* v. *Tinsley*[36] mandamus was found to be a proper remedy to compel school board members to rewrite their minutes for a specified meeting, to show the election of the proper person.

The father-in-law of a married high school student brought mandamus in *State* v. *Marion County Board of Education*[37] to compel her readmission for the balance of the current term from which she had been expelled. The court found the regulation of the board to be reasonable and dismissed the action.

§ 3.5 Setting aside action of the board

In addition to other remedies, including money damages in a proper case, relief may be sought to set aside the action

34 Van Allen v. McCleary, 211 NYS(2d) 501 (NY, 1961).
35 Wagner v. Redmond (La), 127 S(2d) 275 (1960).
36 241 MoApp 690, 236 SW(2d) 24 (1951).
37 202 Tenn 29, 302 SW(2d) 57 (1957).

of the board. In order to set it aside, the action must be invalid and the defect cannot have been cured by subsequent ratification. A common case for nullifying board action is where it acts beyond its authority or in violation of statute or prescribed procedures. Action may be held to be invalid where insufficient notice is given of a special meeting,[38] or where a quorum is lacking.[39]

§ 3.6 Injunction

An injunction is the order of a court of competent jurisdiction commanding or forbidding the doing of certain acts. An injunction may be the only remedy sought or it may be combined with other relief, such as a request for money damages for past loss. Acts within the discretion of the board will not be enjoined unless an abuse of discretion is shown.[40]

An abuse of discretion was defined as follows in *In re Walters' Appeal*:[41]

> A ruling made upon grounds and for reasons clearly untenable constitutes abuse of discretion . . . Abuse of discretion does not necessarily mean ulterior motive, arbitrary conduct or willful disregard of the rights of a litigant, but it may mean a failure to apply principles of law applicable to a situation if prejudice results.

---

[38] Green v. Jones, 144 WVa 276, 108 SE(2d) 1 (1959).

[39] Ibid. In re Walters' Appeal, 270 Wis 561, 72 NW(2d) 535 (1955), it was held that at common law a majority of the members of the board constitutes a quorum and that a majority vote of a quorum is decisive.

[40] School District No. 17 v. Powell, 203 Ore 168, 279 P(2d) 492 (1955), wherein the court stated: "It is properly conceded by the contestant that a school board has a wide discretion in the exercise of the authority committed to it. Courts can interfere only when the board refuses to exercise its authority or pursues some unauthorized course . . . The wisdom or expediency of an act, or the motive with which it is done, is not open to judicial inquiry or consideration where power to do it existed . . . Acts in abuse of discretion may be restrained but the presumption is that there was no abuse . . . ; and the burden of proving abuse of discretion is on the one asserting it, and it must be established by clear and convincing evidence."

[41] 270 Wis 561, at 567, 72 NW(2d) 535 (1955).

The violation of a temporary or permanent injunction order constitutes contempt of court and may be punished accordingly. Among others, the following are situations in which injunctions have been sought against school boards or school board members for alleged delinquencies in record keeping or in following prescribed procedures:

In *Jennings* v. *Clearwater School Dist.*,[42] an injunction was sought to enjoin the issuance of bonds to raise money for purchasing school lots, on the ground that the question had been improperly presented to the voters. The action was dismissed, the court holding that stating the purpose of the vote as for "raising money for purchasing school lots" was sufficient, without designating the actual lots to be purchased.

In *Taylor* v. *Board of Education*,[43] the board was enjoined from constructing a new school on the site of the old in a racially segregated neighborhood. The power to select locations for schools, the court reasoned, must be exercised in accordance with the demands of the federal constitution.

A teacher successfully enjoined a school board from retiring him where the board established an invalid retirement age below that fixed by state statute.[44]

§ 3.7 Actions to remove school board members from office (quo warranto)

The statutes of the state involved must be consulted to determine the proper procedure for removing a public official from office. The traditional remedy of quo warranto has been displaced in some states by a statutory proceeding.

Quo warranto is the legal action normally used to determine the right of a public official to hold his office. The

---

[42] 65 CalApp 102, 223 Pac 84 (1924).

[43] (NY), 191 FSupp 181 (1961).

[44] Herzig v. Board of Education (Conn), 204 A(2d) 827 (1964).

theory and nature of quo warranto is well stated in *State ex inf. McKittrick* v. *Murphy:*[45]

> It is also true that it will lie against a county officer who has been legally elected or appointed to office in the first instance but has forfeited his office by misconduct . . . The officer who violates his oath of office by corruption, wilful misconduct or neglect of official duty automatically loses the right to office and becomes a mere interloper . . . the writ of quo warranto is not a substitute for mandamus or injunction nor for an appeal or writ of error. It is not to be used to prevent an improper exercise of power lawfully possessed. Its purpose is solely to prevent an officer . . . or persons purporting to act as such from usurping a power which they do not have.

The action also is appropriate to test the validity of an election. It was used successfully for this purpose in *State* v. *Consolidated School Dist. No. 3.*[46] The court held that a special election to annex one district to another had been improperly called, since board action had not been taken at a formal meeting. The court noted:

> We think the discussion between the two directors at the clerk's house cannot be dignified as one which fills the requirements of the law . . . The evidence shows that there was no meeting or action of the board in respect to either the March or April election other than the discussion at the clerk's house . . . While there is no question but that the motives of the directors were of the highest, we think their manner of getting together had no more dignity in law than any ordinary fence-row conference.

---

[45] 347 Mo 484, 148 SW(2d) 527, 530 (en banc, 1941). Also see State v. Trent Independent School Dist. (Texas), 141 SW(2d) 438 (1940).

[46] (MoApp), 281 SW(2d) 511 (1955).

In *Commonwealth* v. *King*[47] it was argued that a school board member should be ousted for failing to meet the statutory qualification of an eighth grade education. Although the school records were missing, a teacher's affidavit was accepted as showing that he possessed such an education. The action was dismissed.

The president of the school board was removed from office in *Antoine* v. *McCaffery*[48] for directing that school employees be taken away from work on school projects to do work upon the house of his son, and for paying these employees for such work out of public funds. The court described such action as

> so far out of keeping with the standards of conduct the public has a right to expect from their elected officials . . . as to constitute "gross misconduct" . . . requiring his removal from office.

The validity of the election of board members or of the composition of the board may be attacked in a quo warranto proceeding.[49] In *State* v. *Hensel,*[50] a school board member was removed in a quo warranto proceeding because of a conflict of interest. He owned and operated an employment agency for school teachers. Another ground which was advanced for his removal was overruled. It was held that his violent disagreement with the conduct of the school system, his methods in attempting to enforce his views by appealing to the public, and his personality clashes with other members could not be the basis for his removal from office.

Some states provide a special statutory proceeding for the removal of public officials, including school board members.

---

47 (Ky), 343 SW(2d) 139 (1961).

48 (MoApp), 335 SW(2d) 474 (1960).

49 See Green Mountain School Dist. No. 103 v. Durkee, 56 Wash(2d) 154, 351 P(2d) 525 (1960).

50 (Ohio), 198 NE(2d) 84 (1964).

In Wisconsin, for example, removal of a school board member is by action before the circuit court of the circuit wherein the school district is situated.[51] Illinois permits the county superintendent to remove "any member of a school board from office for wilful failure to perform his official duties."[52] Under Kansas practice the county superintendent, after notice and hearing, declares a forfeiture of a school district officer's office for cause shown.[53] The above examples illustrate the necessity of consulting and following the applicable state statutes on removal, if any.

§ 3.8 Declaration of rights against school board

Tenure and other laws relating to education may establish statutory remedies for the assertion of a teacher's rights against the school board. Such procedures are to be followed where appropriate. Also, the rules of procedure of the state in question may authorize a suit for a declaratory judgment. A declaratory judgment action was brought by a teacher against a school board in Kentucky to determine his rights under the Teachers' Tenure Act.[54] The action was remanded to the trial court with instructions to limit its consideration to records of the board's action.[55]

In *Brooks* v. *School Dist.*[56] a group of Negro schoolteachers brought an action for a declaratory judgment as to whether policies of the board violated their rights under the federal constitution. The court found that they failed to

---

[51] WisStats, sec. 17.13.

[52] IllRevStat 1965, ch. 122, sec. 3-15.5.

[53] KyStatsAnn, sec. 72-1003.

[54] Lewis v. Board of Education (Ky), 348 SW(2d) 921 (1961).

[55] The court observed: "In considering the acts and actions of the board with reference to the employment of Lewis, the rule is that the governing body of a municipal corporation, such as a board of education, can speak only through its records and can confer authority to make or terminate contracts only by proper proceedings at a meeting regularly called and held, when its acts are duly recorded and authenticated."

[56] (Mo), 267 F(2d) 733 (1959).

establish their claim that the failure to renew their contracts resulted from racial discrimination. It stated:

> School boards are vested with wide discretion in matters affecting school management, including the employment of teachers, and a court may not interfere with the board's action unless the board has exercised its powers in an unreasonable, arbitrary, capricious, or unlawful manner.

Negro teachers were sustained in *Alston* v. *School Board,*[57] in which the court declared that they were entitled to the same rate of pay as white teachers. In its decree remanding the case the court held:

> If the allegations of the complaint are established, plaintiffs will be entitled to a declaratory judgment to the effect that the discriminating policy complained of is violative of their rights under the Constitution and to an injunction restraining defendants from making any discrimination on the grounds of race or color in fixing salaries to be paid school teachers after the current fiscal year.

In *Board of Education of Harrodsburg* v. *Bentley,*[58] the Kentucky Court of Appeals set aside a regulation of the school board requiring married students to withdraw from school for one year. The court recognized that the

> government and conduct of public schools, in general, is committed to the discretion of the school board, . . . courts will not interfere with the board's exercise of such discretion unless it appears the board has acted arbitrarily or maliciously.

No maliciousness was found but the regulation was set aside on the ground of arbitrariness.

---

[57] 112 F(2d) 992 (4th Cir. 1940); cert. den., 311 US 693, 61 SCt 75, 85 LEd 448.

[58] (Ky), 383 SW(2d) 677 (1964).

§ 3.9 Actions to recover money misappropriated

While as a general principle public officials are not held civilly liable for payments made in good faith for objects within their jurisdiction, this rule does not apply where a statute limits their discretion, as by directing that teachers' salaries shall conform to a statutory scale. In such instance good faith is not a defense.[59]

§ 3.10 Review of the record of school board action

Under the procedures in some states, action of a school board may be reviewed by the courts by petitioning them for a writ of certiorari. If the writ is granted, the school board submits to the court the records requested, and the judicial review is of such records. In *Bray* v. *Barry*,[60] the court in such a proceeding reviewed the action of a school board in suspending a teacher. The court upheld the suspension, determining that a majority of a quorum of the board could act, even though one or two vacancies on the board had not been filled.

In some states a review of board action is permitted to the state board of education, such as the proceeding in New York under Article 78.

§ 3.11 Conclusion

From the above discussion it is hoped that several conclusions are clear. First, the law pertaining to schools and school personnel is state and not federal law. It therefore varies somewhat from state to state, often in accordance with differences in statutory codes relating to education. It will have been noted, for example, that with reference to school records as evidence, some courts do not permit outside evidence to determine board action, some do so in ex-

---

[59] See Golding v. Latimer, 239 Miss 163, 121 S(2d) 615 (1960).

[60] 91 RI 34, 160 A(2d) 577 (1960).

ceptional cases, and others do so freely. The law of each state must therefore be consulted in each instance.

A second general conclusion which must be drawn is that while school boards and school board members are subject to suit at the whim of a plaintiff, such suits are not successful unless school board members have been guilty of some wrongful conduct, or have failed to follow statutory or other legal requirements or procedures.

A third generalization is that school board members must familiarize themselves with such requirements and procedures and act within legal bounds, which in the case of discretionary acts are not very restrictive, but which are exacting where ministerial acts are involved. If a statute directs a school board to follow certain procedures, or to do or refrain from doing certain acts, the school board member must be impressed with the fact that such statute is to be obeyed.

A fourth conclusion is that the school board attorney has a vital role to play in the process of administering the affairs of the complicated business of modern education.

Chapter 4

SCHOOL BOARD COMMUNICATIONS

by

THOMAS A. SHANNON

Attorney-at-law; legal counsel, San Diego Unified School District, San Diego, California; member of the California Bar, the Minnesota Bar, and admitted to the practice of law in the United States Supreme Court.

Chapter 4

SCHOOL BOARD COMMUNICATIONS

§ 4.1 Introduction

As a governmental entity, a school board receives many communications from citizens on subjects which vary widely, depending on the time of the year and the matters currently before the board. These communications come from residents of the school district who have strong personal or business interests in the deliberations of the board or from others whose interests, while as intense, are more general in nature. Both groups communicate with the school board on the premise that the board, as a governmental entity, will consider their communication. They realize that the school board must expect the political and legal consequences which could flow from a refusal to consider a communication which is presented to the board by any citizen or group of citizens.

The political consequences of a school board's refusal to consider communications from citizens are quite obvious. The refusal may be made the basis of a recall election in those states where the recall is a device to remove from office those board members with whom a majority of the electors in the school district are dissatisfied.[1] It also may be a plank in the platform of a citizen attempting to unseat a board member who joined in the refusal to consider the communication. Other political ramifications, which go to the heart of the operation and very existence of the school district, are also possible. These would include using the refusal to marshal opposition against school tax increase elections, school bond elections, and elections to unify several independent school districts into one or to fragment one school district into several, in the announced interest of bettering local education.

There is also an overriding political consideration which must be taken into account in our democracy. It is no secret that the proper functioning of our free society depends in large measure upon an informed citizenry. In recent years, great public interest has been focused on public education. Matters which used to be discussed only in the teacher lounges at school are now bandied about with the color of deep authority in restaurants and living rooms. This revolution in public attitude, generally attributed to "Sputnik" and conditioned by a post-World War II rise in the general education level of the population, has manifested itself in many states by laws which require school boards to conduct their deliberations and make their decisions openly in public. While the requirement that deliberations and actions of the school board be public may not be linked firmly to a school board policy of actually consider-

---

[1] The state legislature establishes grounds for recall of school board members. Many states require no particular grounds for recall. For example, sec. 1135 of the California Education Code simply states: "The recall petition shall contain a statement of not more than 200 words of the specific grounds on which the recall is sought, for the information of the voters."

No listing of grounds for recall is made by the California legislature. The only restriction on recall in California is that a recall petition may not be circulated or filed during the first six-month period of a school board member's term of office or during the six-month period immediately prior to the time at which the regular election would be held for his office.

ing communications at public meeting, the philosophy of such laws would seem to embrace both ideas. This philosophy is well expressed in the preamble to California's Ralph M. Brown Act, which declares, in pertinent part:

> The people of this state do not yield their sovereignty to the agencies which serve them. The people, in delegating authority, do not give their public servants the right to decide what is good for the people to know and what is not good for them to know. The people insist on remaining informed so that they may retain control over the instruments they have created.[2]

As a practical matter, it is difficult to comprehend how a school board, which wields an authority delegated to it by the people, could in the absence of a most compelling reason, refuse to consider a communication from even one of that mass of our citizenry collectively called "the people," which comprises the repository of all political power in our democracy.

§ 4.2 Right of petition—First Amendment

The refusal by the board to consider citizens' communications also could have serious legal consequences, depending on the nature of the communication and the manner in which it is proposed to be presented.

The First Amendment to the United States Constitution declares:

> Congress shall make no law respecting an establishment of religion, or prohibiting the free exercise thereof; or abridging the freedom of speech, or of the press; or the right of the people peaceably to assemble, and to *petition the government for a redress of grievances.* (Emphasis added.)

---

[2] Sec. 54950, California Government Code.

A cursory reading of this amendment might seem to indicate that for the right of petition to come into play against the federal government, an "assembly" must first have been held. However, the right of petition is considerably more expansive than that quick assumption.

In the first place, the First Amendment has been made applicable to the states by the Fourteenth Amendment to the United States Constitution.[3] A school board generally is an instrumentality of the state and, therefore, the rights guaranteed by the First Amendment have full force and effect against school boards.

Nor does the right of petition depend on a prior "assembly."[4] In 1941, the Supreme Court of the United States upheld the right of petition in circumstances involving a telegram addressed to the United States Secretary of Labor, vehemently criticizing the action of a state court in a pending case.[5] Today, lobbying is regarded as a primary expression of the right of petition.[6] The right is not limited to a "redress of grievances,"

> but comprehends demands for an exercise by the government of its powers in furtherance of the interests and prosperity of the petitioners, and of their views on politically contentious matters.[7]

It is quite possible today that a court would hold that the right to petition imposes upon the school board a correlative duty to at least "consider" communications which it receives from citizens. It could be strongly argued that a refusal by a school board, or its delegated representative, to

---

[3] De Jonge v. Oregon, 299 US 353 (1937); Herndon v. Lowry, 301 US 242 (1937).

[4] United States v. Cruikshank, 92 US 542 (1876).

[5] Bridges v. California, 314 US 252, 86 LEd 192, 62 SCt 190 (1941).

[6] The Constitution of the United States of America, Analysis and Interpretation, Legislative Reference Service, Library of Congress, Edwin S. Corwin, Ed., 1953 (p. 810).

[7] Id., p. 806.

consider a communication emasculates the right of petition guaranteed by the United States Constitution. If this correlative duty does exist,[8] any violation of it by a school board or a protective school administrator could be made the grounds for a legal action brought to remove from office or otherwise punish the offending parties.

In addition to the First Amendment, a state constitutional provision or state law might specifically impose the duty on a school board to receive and consider certain communications from school district employees and citizens.

§ 4.3 Board policy

It seems clear, therefore, that a policy instituting an orderly system of receiving communications and channeling them to the school board should be developed in school districts. The policy should be in writing and should be sufficiently broad and flexible to permit the application of discretion in determining which communications are appropriate for administrative action on a lower-than-school-board level, and which communications are more properly the concern of the school board.

In a survey of twenty-nine of the larger school districts in the United States, conducted by the author in August, 1964, a majority indicated that no written policy governing the handling of communications to the school board was in effect. Each of the responding school boards, however, had a definite practice for the handling of such communications. The practices, or unwritten policies, varied widely among school boards, as did the provisions of the written policies.

---

[8] The California attorney general apparently is of the persuasion that a citizen has a right to be heard by a board of education on questions being considered by a board, and that an unwarranted restriction on this right in the form of requiring a representative of a citizens' organization to submit a list of members to the board as a condition precedent to addressing the board is invalid, as an infringement on the constitutionally protected right of association and free speech. OpsCal AttyGen No. 65-146 (July 15, 1965).

§ 4.4 Handling of board communications

The general approach to handling school board communications, which is set either through written policy or established practice, seems to take two forms: (1) communications are initially reviewed by the superintendent and their disposition is determined by the superintendent as the chief administrative officer of the school board, or (2) communications are received by the school board secretary or clerk and their disposition is handled either under the administrative control of the superintendent, in those school districts where the superintendent is responsible for the administration of the school board office, or in close liaison with him in those school districts where the school board secretary or clerk is answerable only to the school board.

Any policy governing school board communications may be analyzed by considering the significant attributes of the generic term "communications." A careful look at the word "communications" would seem to indicate that it may be viewed as follows:

1. Type of communication
2. Source of communication
3. Substance of communication
4. Response to communication
5. Communication as a "public record"

Considering each of these elements, *in seriatim,* should reveal the great diversity of school board communications and the problems of avoiding or minimizing the legal and political dangers inherent in the handling of communications addressed to school boards.

§ 4.5 Type of communication

Any communication to the school board is obviously either written or verbal. Assuming that a written communication is appropriate for school board consideration, it may be channeled to the school board with ease and simplicity.

It may be summarized in digest form or simply mechanically duplicated before forwarding to individual school board members.

Generally, mechanical duplication would appear more desirable because it is clearly cheaper. It does not involve high-priced legal or administrative talent in drafting the summary and is not subject to later criticism by the writer that the summary took words out of context or misplaced the emphasis of the communication. Viewed from a standpoint of administrative efficiency, mechanical duplication of communications to the board can be routinized, and virtually all of the work in making sure the communications reach the board members can be done by clerical personnel.

A verbal communication is not handled so easily. A telephone call of protest or advice by a citizen presents practical complications. If it is not a request for a "public hearing" before the school board, the school board member or administrator must decide on an *ad hoc* basis the most practical way of dealing with the matter. Clearly, if the subject of the verbal request involves an administrative act, and if that act may be made without prior school board consideration, and the judgment of the superintendent is that such act should be made, the verbal communication never officially comes before the school board. However, where the matter is one deserving school board attention, the recipient of the verbal communication must decide whether he desires to place it before the school board or require the citizen making the verbal communication either to "put it in writing" or appear before the school board for a "public hearing."

A decision that the citizen reduce his thoughts to writing should represent a balance between, on the one hand, being a "message carrier" to the school board, with its attendant dangers of presenting a garbled version of the message, and, on the other hand, the natural desire of school boards to avoid the appearance that it is the type of bureaucracy which operates only through the typewriter rolls.

A decision that the citizen himself present his communication personally to the school board requires an interpretation of the school board policy or practice and of the provisions of state law governing "public hearings." In some states, the state law requires or permits "public hearings" at a school board meeting on subjects such as adoption of the budget, school district reorganization, personnel, and student discipline matters. Individual school boards may have similar policies.

Where a school board operates on a committee basis, the presentation might more appropriately be made to a committee. Regardless of whether the hearing is before a committee or the school board as a whole, certain restrictions may be applied to the presentation. These include the imposition of a reasonable time limit on the speaker, a requirement that the speaker identify himself and his interest in the topic about which he proposes to speak, and the rule of relevancy, which serves to keep the speaker on the course of his subject matter.

It should be noted that unless state law otherwise provides, a school board has the legal discretionary power to refuse to turn its meetings into a public forum for citizens.[9] The constitutional right to petition would probably not be extended to such length that a school board would be required to hear in "public hearing" at board meetings any citizen who merely desired to be heard only in that way. A "petition" may take many forms and it is doubtful that the courts would permit a citizen to choose his own particular way of petitioning. More likely, the courts would uphold the school board's exercise of discretion if the school board could show that there is an alternate channel of communication or petition open for citizens who wish to present a viewpoint to the school board.

---

[9] Ibid.

§ 4.6 Source of communication

Considering the school district as the focus of communications to the school board, there are two sources of such communications: the internal source, which encompasses communications to the school board from within the school district, and the external source, which broadly includes all other communications.

The first and only official internal source of communication to the school board is the administration of the school district, epitomized in most school districts by the superintendent of schools and in other school districts by the superintendent and some other administrator, such as the business manager. Communications from these offices are officially made at school board meetings and are coupled with administrative recommendations for school board action.

In addition to communications from the administration, there are two other internal sources of communications. In some states, the law requires that school boards deal directly with employee organizations on matters affecting salary, hours, and other conditions of employment. In the absence of state law, a school board may choose to deal directly with its employees. In either case, the school board must afford equal treatment to all employees and employee organizations, unless a collective bargaining or a professional negotiation type agreement is in effect.

Occasionally, an individual employee will send a communication to the school board. This is the second source of those internal communications which do not originate in school district administration offices. Since most employees are also citizens, such communications sometimes demand that a decision be made on the issue of whether the employee is communicating in his capacity as an employee or in his role as citizen. The courts have consistently said that employment by a school district in no way affects a citizen's right of free speech to speak out on school matters, providing that his public utterances do not adversely affect the instructional program or prejudice the good order and discipline of the schools. Less difficulty is encountered when the employee submits a laudatory communication to the school board. Common courtesy would seem to require that the school board members each be made aware of the communication, but courtesy need not be extended so far that the communication must be placed on the public agenda. When communications of this type receive publicity through the agenda, other employees similarly situated might wish not to be outdone in their expressions of approval for school board actions with which they are pleased.

A veritable "love letter" correspondence can begin which can have a negative impact on the morale of those employees who view such public communications as nothing more than self-serving declarations.

In many school districts, the school board operates on a committee system. Some school boards have established an elaborate structure of permanent committees which are charged with the responsibility of considering specific areas of school board concern. Many school boards use the committee system only on a casual, *ad hoc* basis. Other school boards, acting on the theory that a board committee tends to undermine the administrative authority of the superintendent, especially in those cases where the committee's findings are not in tune with the recommendations of the superintendent, choose never to form a committee of its own members but, rather, rely exclusively on the administration to do all of the research and preparation incident to a school board decision.

School board committee communications are more in the nature of communications *from* the school board than *to* the school board. Technically, therefore, they are not "internal communications," in the sense that the term is used in this discussion. School boards which have permanent committees may operate either independently of the superintendent or in close liaison with him. If they actively cooperate with the superintendent, opponents of the "committee system" argue that the committee is merely performing an administrative fact-finding chore and is meeting only because the school board places more trust in findings made by board members than it does in the findings of administrators who are insulated from the school board (and its pressures from citizens) by the superintendent. On the other hand, proponents of the school board "committee system" insist that the board committee is an eloquent example of democracy in action. They argue that the elected representatives of the people can maintain policy control of the schools only by "digging into the problem areas of education" and that this can be done best through school board committees which tend to place board members in the vanguard of educational policy making. They also declare that they aid the superintendent by placing a buffer between him and the public, especially in extremely controversial areas of school concern where public acceptance is crucial, such as "de facto segregation," location of school attendance boundaries, and school tax or bond elections, to name only a few. In the final analysis, the existence or nonexistence of a school board "committee system" depends as much upon the character, custom, and political history of the community which a school board serves, as upon the rationales described above.

Regardless of the merits of school board committees, their communications for the entire school board present the problem of whether or not the superintendent will support the communications. The superintendent should be given the opportunity to carefully analyze the communication before it is made public at a school board meeting. If he supports the communication, there is no problem. However, if he does not, it would seem that, as the chief administrative officer of the *entire* board, he should be given adequate time to present his own position on the matter. The school board is then placed in the unenviable position of deciding between the two proposals, but this is probably considerably better than rash acceptance of one proposed course of action over another course of action which, though not carefully explored at the time of decision, might prove later to have been superior.

Communications from sources external to the school district come either from the general public or from those persons and organizations who have entered into a special relationship with the school board. Communications from the general public usually are placed on the public meeting agenda, if the substance of the communications seems to warrant such handling. It is a matter of administrative discretion whether communications from other external sources, such as school board associations, citizen committees,[10] construction or maintenance contractors, and con-

---

[10] A citizen committee acts in lieu of a school board committee as a quasi-"agent" of the community to find facts and make recommendations on matters on which the school board desires community study on a broader base than that which the board believes itself capable of giving. Communications from citizen committees could be managed by the following sample rule and regulation, which, of course, is subject to alteration as the local conditions dictate:

"The board of education may appoint citizens of the community to serve on citizen committees for the purpose of counseling and advising the board of education on matters pertaining to the government of the district. Citizens so appointed shall receive no monetary compensation nor expense reimbursement. The names of citizens proposed for appointment to citizen committees may be considered and tentatively selected in private executive session of the board of education, provided, however, that final and official selection of persons appointed to such citizen committees shall be made in public meeting of the board of education. Citizen committees appointed by the board of education act in a purely counseling and advisory capacity and their findings and recommendations are not binding upon the board of education.

"All findings and recommendations of citizen committees, including minority reports, shall be submitted to the board as a communication, and shall appear as such on a public agenda of the meeting of the board of education held next after receipt of the communication by the board. If a citizen committee communication challenges the personal capacity of an employee to render service to this board, involves a school district matter being litigated in the courts, or concerns the reputation of a pupil or former pupil of this school district, it shall *not* be placed

sultants, to mention but a few, should be made a part of the meeting agenda. The general rule for determining a suitable course of action would appear to be bifurcated:

> (1) Is school board action made necessary by the communication? or (2) Is this a matter which deserves public attention by the school board?

§ 4.7 Substance of communication

It is apparent that regardless of the type and source of the communication, the principal determinant of whether a communication deserves the attention of the school board, either privately or by inclusion in the public meeting agenda, is the *substance* of the communication. The public views its school board as a personification of its school district. Attorneys and experienced businessmen, for more sophisticated reasons, generally share the public's view, with the result that much correspondence of the school district is addressed to the school board. The problem which is posed is how to differentiate between communications which should be taken care of by the administration and which should have the attention of the school board.

Good administrative practice dictates that matters should be handled at the lowest possible level where appropriate action may be taken. A school board is a policy-making body which serves the primary function of governing the school district at the local level. Once the school board has adopted a policy on a particular subject, the administration is

---

on the public agenda. Instead, such communication shall be offered for private consideration of the board at an executive session which shall be held following the meeting of the board next after receipt of the communication by the board.

"The superintendent is enjoined to make available immediately any information to the citizen committee concerning the government of the district which such citizen committee from time to time may request in the course and scope of fulfilling their charge from the board of education. Nothing in this section shall be construed to prohibit the employment of professional consultants as permitted in law by the board of education."

charged with the implementation of the policy. If the communication challenges the policy, or its implementation, of course the school board would wish to be made aware of the communication. If, however, the communication seems to presume that the policy is valid and makes no quarrel with the implementation, there is no reason to believe that the school board would be interested in it. These communications are concerned with administrative detail, which is the appropriate province of the administration hired by the school board. When the school board deals with such matters, the delicate policy/administration balance is disturbed. A disturbance of this balance, if not brought back to equilibrium by the school board, could result in a confused and demoralized administration. This situation corrects itself either through the voluntary or forced removal of the chief administrator or through the inculcation of a deplorable timidity in the administration. This timidity is manifested by the channeling of administrative minutiae through the school board, thus confounding sound administrative practice and robbing the school board of precious time to consider more fully the overriding matters of importance inherent in educational policy-making.

A communication dealing with routine matters, even though addressed to the school board, should be immediately referred to the administration for action. However, when communications deal with policy, or challenge the implementation of policy, the school board should be involved. This involvement may be effected by either reporting the communication directly to the school board at its meeting on the "communications" section of the agenda, or introducing it through another section of the agenda and incorporating it with an administrative recommendation for school board action.

It sometimes happens that the school board will receive communications which on their face appear to be appropriate for board consideration but which include, as part of the substance of the communications, matters which may be defamatory in nature or which involve charges against school district employees. These communications deserve special handling because of their legal ramifications.

A communication lodging a charge against an employee of the school district must be carefully analyzed to ascertain whether the complaint is aimed at the employee's discharge of his employment duties and responsibilities, or at his personal character or fitness to perform his duties and carry out his responsibilities. If only his performance is at issue in the communication, it is probably fair game in the public hunting ground, and no particular legal risk is run in presenting the communication to the school board in public meeting. If, however, the communication challenges his personal capacity to perform, a different situation is presented. Many states have legislation which either require a private hearing before the school board on charges and complaints brought against employees, or give the employee an option to choose between a private or public hearing.[11] A communication containing a charge or complaint against an employee, if published as a part of the public agenda, could result in a lawsuit, grounded in the tort of defamation and the violation of specific state legislation against the school board or its members personally, and the recovery of substantial money damages, depending on the nature of the communication.

As a practical matter, it is often difficult to distinguish between a charge against an employee's performance and his personal capacity to perform. If the communication is addressed to the school board, the wise administrator will submit it to the school board. If he has doubts as to the appropriateness of making the communication public, he and the school board would do well to treat the matter as confidential, sit back and let the sender of the communication make it public, if that is the concern of the sender. Any

[11] See sec. 54957, California, Government Code.

lawsuit arising out of these ashes will pit the employee against the sender, and the school board would probably only be featured in the role of a witness-spectator.

Communications directed to the school board may be defamatory in nature without involving school district employees. In these cases, the problem is not complicated by state legislation protecting school district employees. The issue becomes one of pure tort law in the area of defamation. Generally, the tort of defamation involves an invasion of plaintiff's interest in his reputation by defendant's communication to others of matters tending to hold plaintiff up to hatred, contempt, or ridicule, or to cause him to be shunned or avoided, or to injure him in his occupation.[12]

In order for defamation to be actionable in a court of law, there must be a "publication" of the defamatory communication. A "publication" first occurs when the defamatory material is communicated by the initial defamer to another person, and generally continues to occur each time any person repeats it. In other words, liability could attach itself to each repeater of the defamatory statement, unless the repeater stands in a special position in the law. In this sense, a school board, or its members, could be liable for making public the defamatory communications of others, even though the school board did not participate in the actual framing of the defamatory statement.

Whether or not a publication of a school board communication through the medium of the school board public meeting agenda will give rise to liability depends on an analysis of tort law as it could apply to the school board in those circumstances. The question of tort liability for defamation varies from state to state, and the school board should request from its attorney administrative guidelines on defamation to obviate as much as possible the difficulties

---

[12] See cases collected at sec. 3, "Libel and Slander," Vol. 33, American Jurisprudence.

which can arise even from an honest ignorance of the law. Because school districts are "wealthy" governmental entities and have the obvious capacity to pay substantial money damages, and because school board members are often persons of economic substance in their communities, school boards and individual board members make "good defendants," especially where the original defamer is a person of limited financial resources.

However, it is much easier to file a lawsuit than it is to obtain a verdict and collect on a judgment. As Professor Reynolds C. Seitz has said:

> Actually, on the statistical level, the danger of school men incurring money damage for defamatory utterances is not high. In a very significant number of instances the school man who communicates defamatory material will unknowingly act within the protection of a privilege. At other times his defamatory utterances may be merely the type of slander which does not cause the defamed to suffer the money damages which the courts demand as a basis for recovery. Furthermore, the calculated risk is good that many parents will not sue the teachers and administrators.[13]

While these remarks were directed at employees of school boards, the observations would retain considerable validity if aimed at school board members.

There are two aspects of defamation in connection with school board communications. The first may be viewed as the receipt by the school board of the defamatory communication. At this point, there has been a "publication" by the defamer to the school board. If the letter goes no further than the school board and its agents, the school board is merely a passive witness and has no real concern over its

---

[13] Law and the School Principal, Vol. 3, p. 151 of Legal Problems of Education Series sponsored by the National Organization on Legal Problems of Education, Seitz, Ed., W. H. Anderson Co., 1961.

own tort liability for defamation. It is in the position of a receiver of defamatory utterances and would be involved in any legal action over the communications merely as a witness.

The second aspect of the problem may be considered as beginning with receipt of the communication and continuing through the period of dissemination of the communication to others not school board members. It is this "publication" with which we are most concerned.

The "publication" of defamatory communications can be made by school board members in three ways: (1) while deliberating in private meeting of "executive session" as part of the board, (2) while deliberating in public meeting as part of the board, and (3) while outside of a board meeting and acting as an individual board member or private citizen.

The first two kinds of "publications" by school board members may be analyzed together. Usually, either an absolute or a conditional privilege would protect a school board, and a school board member, from tort liability.[14] An absolute privilege, in those states where it is recognized, would save a board member from liability even when the board member revealed the contents of a board communication through malicious motive or when there was no basis to believe it to be true. A conditional privilege, which most school boards enjoy, is somewhat different. This kind of privilege holds that a member of a school board cannot take advantage of his official position to give expression to private defamation against another. In short, if the privilege is abused for malicious purposes, such misconduct is actionable at law. It could be said that this privilege is extended to school board members "on condition" that it be used with good faith in service of the ideal for which a

[14] See cases collected at secs. 131, and 144, "Libel and Slander," Vol. 33, American Jurisprudence. See also 40 ALR(2d) 951; Kelley v. Dunne, 344 F(2d) 129 (1st Cir., 1965).

"privilege" for legislative bodies exist, namely: to permit untrammeled inquiry into all matters of public concern by public officers acting as part of a legislative body.

The third kind of "publication" puts the school board member in the same shoes as a strictly private citizen. That is, if the school board member reveals a defamatory communication outside of a board meeting, he has "published" it and could be held liable. No privilege extends to this conduct because the courts have not found that any useful social purpose would be served in permitting a member of a legislative body to reveal defamatory materials outside of the legislative meeting room, which the law views as the place where such revelations are supposed to have social utility.[15]

Whether or not the defense of "truth" will apply depends primarily on the statute or constitutional provisions in the individual state[16] In some states truth is an absolute defense, and in others only a conditional privilege which evaporates if the statement is not published with good motives and for justifiable ends. A school board member depends on the accuracy of the letter writer, when he releases the contents of a board communication. The wise board member will consider that carefully while contemplating future reliance on the defense of truth.

§ 4.8 Response to communication

Every letter to the board of education deserves a response. The foundation upon which this principle rests is the plain rule of courtesy that when a citizen makes a statement or inquiry about his schools, he should not be ignored. This courtesy is given special color because of the fact that a school district is a governmental entity. If the letter objects to a policy of the board, or challenges the

---

[15] Coffin v. Coffin, 4 Mass 1, 3 AmDec 189 (1808). See also cases collected at sec. 141, Vol. 33, American Jurisprudence.

[16] Sec. 44 et seq., California Civil Code.

implementation of a policy, it should be answered in writing by the board. If the letter is within the administrative province as discussed earlier, the administration should be allowed to respond in any manner it sees fit, on the theory that the letter is merely part of the discretionary area delegated by the board. Because the administration is responsible to the school board in all matters of administrative discretion, the board has an adequate check on the appropriateness of the response.

Careful judgment must be exercised in framing a written response by the board to any letter it receives. The signer of the letter should be a person who is either directly or indirectly responsible to the people of the school district. In short, the signer should be an elected or appointed member of the school board. Usually, the signer should be the board president, secretary, or clerk. Regardless of whether the recipient of the board's letter is in agreement with the response, he will at least be confident that his communication actually reached the highest level of school political responsibility, which the board is viewed to be by the public. He will not have even the vague feeling, erroneous and unfair as it might be, that his "message" was sidetracked or "watered down" by some "insensitive bureaucratic administrator trying to keep the board brainwashed as to what is really going on in the community."

Each written response of the board must be complete in itself. The opening paragraph of the response should carefully restate the message of the citizen in the precise terms which the board understood it. Candor should be the principle characteristic of the restatement. If the citizen writer is protesting or complaining about something, the protest or complaint should be labeled as such.

If possible, the crucial wording of the citizen letter writer should be paraphrased using, wherever appropriate, the exact wording of the citizen letter writer in quotations. This technique serves two important ends: (1) it insures that the board clearly understood the import of the citizen letter writer, and (2) it places the substance of the board's reply, contained in subsequent paragraphs, in proper perspective. The latter point is especially important, because many citizen letter writers are not entirely precise in their statements. If the school board letter fails to identify the real issue, it may be used as a response to a myriad of vaguely phrased charges listed in the citizen's letter. This often leads to gross misinterpretation of the board's letter and is a potential political weapon which may be used against the board. As any school board member well knows, misunderstandings are difficult to clear up in the public arena, especially where there may not be complete good faith, as there seldom is in controversial political matters. Additionally, the board's letter is often seen by persons who have not had the opportunity of seeing the letter of the citizen which prompted the board's response.

The substance of the board's response must be carefully prepared. It must, on the one hand, give a clear and definite response to the citizen letter writer and, on the other hand, not necessarily operate to bind the board's hands in future similar matters.

If the school board's letter response is not officially adopted by the board, of course it cannot "bind" the board in any legal sense. A school board may only act as a board; no individual member may "bind" the board unless there is a grant of express authorization by the board on a matter which has been approved by the board.[17] And then, if no contract is involved, the board would be bound only until such time as it decides to "unbind" itself by a change in policy. But there is another, perhaps more important consideration than the strictly "legal" consideration. The practical political reality is that the president, secretary or clerk of the board may actually "bind" the board as far as the citizen is concerned. This "binding" is in the nature of the

[17] Sec. 46.07, McQuillan, Municipal Corporations (3d ed.).

much-joked-about political "campaign promise." When a responsible official of the board signs his name to a school board letter, the public views such act in the same light as it would look upon a signed letter from any other person representing a group. The overriding "reasoning" is: "a signed letter is a signed letter is a signed letter, on and on . . . " The legal nicety of what binds a board is simply wind in the treetops.

It appears, therefore, that the board's reply, while being direct must also be general in nature. It must be drafted much like a constitutional provision. While addressing itself specifically to the particular issue presented, its treatment must be sufficiently broad in nature that it will not come back to haunt the board in future deliberations where a decision on a similar matter is necessary, but where the individual facts are sufficiently different to demand a response emphatic of different elements.

§ 4.9 Communication as a public record

When a communication to the school board is filed with the board it becomes a matter of official record. Simply because it is part of the official record, however, does not necessarily mean that it is a public record open to public inspection. Whether a communication is available for inspection by members of the public depends on state law. Some states provide expressly for confidentiality in privileged communications statutes. These statutes are strictly construed. That is, they are read literally and marginal cases will be resolved in favor of public inspection.

Many state courts recognize a common-law right in citizens to inspect all matters of public record, except where the right is curtailed by the legislature because the public interest in confidentiality outweighs the interest of the citizens seeking disclosure. It should be emphasized that:

> the fact that an examination of the books and records would cause worry and inconvenience or that the citi-

zen making application for examination is politically hostile to the administration is no excuse for denial.[18]

In the absence of statute, what constitutes a public record open to examination is a question of law and will be resolved by the courts through a consideration of the nature of the record, custom and usage, and a balancing of the public and private interests involved.[19] A school board asserting the privilege, under statute or otherwise, has the burden of showing that records kept by a public body are confidential and are not subject to disclosure.[20]

Where disclosure is the rule, a correlative right exists to make copies. However, the right of disclosure and copymaking is subject to reasonable rules and regulations of the school board governing the time and manner of examination, the security of the records, and the prior right to the use of the records by the public body.[21] It should be noted that secreting public records could be a criminal offense or grounds for impeachment from office of the public official who deliberately conceals his records and acts as if they did not exist.[22]

External communications, or communications filed with a school board from sources outside the school district officials, are almost always matters of open public record, subject to examination by citizens if the communications do not involve charges against employees or pupils. If charges

---

[18] Id., sec. 14.14.

[19] New York Post Corp. v. Moses, 210 NYS(2d) 88, 12 AppDiv(2d) 243 (1961). Even where there is a "confidential communications" statute, the wording may be so general that action to withhold a document based on protection of the statute must be very carefully considered. For example, section 1881, California Code of Civil Procedure broadly states: "5. (Public Officers) A public officer cannot be examined as to communications made to him in official confidence, when the public interest would suffer by the disclosure."

[20] Sears, Roebuck & Co. v. Hoyt, 107 NYS(2d) 756, 202 Misc 43 (1951); Gallagher v. Boller, 231 CalApp –, 231 ACA (No. 5) 537 (1965).

[21] Lee v. Beach Pub. Co., 127 Fla 600, 173 So 440 (1937).

[22] State v. Harrison, 130 WVa 246, 43 SE(2d) 214 (1947).

against employees and pupils are the proper subject of private school board meetings or "executive session" under state law or school board policy, it would seem that disclosure of such records should be resisted.

There is virtually no case law on the right of examination of "internal communications," or communications from the administration or individual employees of the school board. When personnel or individual pupil matters are not the subject of such communications, it would appear that communications from the superintendent or other employees are at least in the category of public business. If the subject of the communication is considered confidential by the sender, the communication is generally not "filed" with the school board in any formal sense. Rather, it is sent to each school board member personally. If the school board member who receives a copy of such communication does not wish to reveal its contents upon demand by a citizen who discovers its existence, he might refer the citizen to the sender. Should the sender refuse to divulge the contents, the citizen may seek discovery by mandamus, which is a legal action to compel the doing of a certain act. In this case, mandamus would attempt to require the school board member or sender of the communication to permit him to inspect the withheld communication. As noted earlier, the burden of proof that the record sought is privileged will be on the person insisting upon its confidentiality.

Generally, state law does not concern itself with the saving and storage of communications to the school board. The state legislature or state board of education seems content if only a proper record of local school board proceedings are kept. Therefore, it is usually up to the school board to provide for the storage and filing of communications which it receives in the regular course of its business as the trustees of public education.

Except for those communications which school board members expressly request to be made "a part of the record," it is probably best that communications to school boards be kept for a minimum of three years. It is important that the school board adopt a policy governing the length of filing time which communications should be kept. In the event of a legal action where such communications could play a part, it is embarrassing to the administration when it cannot produce the desired communication because it was destroyed by an act of administrative discretion.

§ 4.10 Conclusion

A school board is a local government agency. It must be responsive to the electorate or it will not be able to sustain itself in the role of trustee of public education. While responsiveness certainly does not mean capitulation to every demand presented to the school board, it should embrace a guarantee that at least every communication presented to it will be fully and carefully considered. A school board can insure that petitioning citizens will be heard by the adoption of a policy governing the handling of communications to the school board. Moreover, the conscientious administrator, who is charged with the responsibility of deciding whether each particular communication deserves the attention of the school board, will cheer the adoption of a board policy covering the subject, because it will give him firm ground on which to anchor his decision.

Not every communication deserves the personal attention of the school board. Some communications are routine administrative matters. A general rule is that communications should be handled at the lowest appropriate level and as expeditiously as possible, because it is the *result* which citizens are concerned about. Regardless of the level on which the communication is handled, a reply in the name and on behalf of the school board should be given. Any reply must be precisely phrased so as not to embarrass the school board in later similar situations.

Special attention must be given to communications which

are potentially defamatory in nature. As a practical matter, the thing to look for in defamation is a personal attack on the reputation of any person or business firm working for the school board.

Communications filed with the school board are matters of public record and are available for public examination unless the school board can show good cause why the communications should be confidential. The school board should decide how long it requires that communications should be saved.

Communications to the school board are the most significant link between the citizens of a school district and their school board. The board must assert its dominion over its communications by the adoption and implementation of its own policy, or run the risk of serious political embarrassment or possible legal action.[23]

---

[23] Sample school board rules and regulations governing communications appear below and at note 10. These samples may be changed to fit local conditions as the reader desires.

Written Communications to the Board

All written communications addressed to the board of education involving policy matters which are properly the first concern of the board of education shall be placed on the public agenda of the meeting of the board of education held next after receipt of the written communication by the board. If a written communication challenges the personal capacity of an employee to render service to this board, involves a school district matter being litigated in the courts, or concerns the reputation of a pupil or former pupil of this school district, it shall not be placed on the public agenda. Instead, such communication shall be offered for private consideration of the board at an executive session which shall be held following the meeting of the board next after receipt of the written communication by the board. The board may establish deadline times prior to a meeting, at which communications to be considered at that meeting, or following that meeting in "executive session," must be submitted.

Scheduled Hearings

All requests by citizens for a scheduled hearing before the board of education shall be placed on the public agenda of the meeting of the board held next after receipt of the request by the board. The agenda shall contain the name and address of the person requesting a scheduled hearing, his representative capacity, if any, and a brief description of the subject on which the person requesting a scheduled hearing desires to be heard. The board of education shall decide at each meeting by majority vote of the members voting whether or not it shall hear the person requesting a scheduled hearing. If a request for a public hearing challenges the personal capacity of an employee to render service to this board, involves a school district matter being litigated in the courts, or concerns the reputation of a pupil or former pupil of this school district, it shall not be placed on the public agenda. Instead, the speaker shall be offered an opportunity to be heard in a private executive session of the board which shall be held following the meeting of the board next after receipt of the request for hearing by the board. The board may establish deadline times prior to a meeting, at which requests for scheduled hearings to be considered at that meeting must be made.

Unscheduled Hearings

The board of education shall decide at each meeting by majority vote of the members voting whether or not it shall hear persons requesting an unscheduled hearing before the board of education. If held, such unscheduled hearings shall be heard at the conclusion of the meeting as provided in the "order of business" of the public agenda. An unscheduled hearing may be interrupted at any time on motion of any one member of the board. If interrupted, the board, by majority vote, shall then decide whether it should continue to hear the speaker in public meeting, whether it should hear the speaker in private executive session, or whether it should refuse to continue hearing the speaker at all. . . .

Disposition of Requests Made During Public Hearing

The board of education shall decide the disposition of questions or requests for information which are made by citizens at a public hearing before the board. The board shall vote on such disposition during the public meeting at which the public hearing was granted. If the board fails to take such action, no response to the citizen other than that which is made during the meeting is necessary.

Written Record of Board Proceedings

The official records of proceedings of board of education meetings shall be known as the minutes. The minutes shall be a record only of actions taken by the board of education, except that any member or the superintendent may direct that his remarks, or a summary thereof, made during a meeting, be included in the minutes. The minutes shall be approved by the board of education at any subsequent meeting by majority vote of the members voting at the meeting at which such proposal for approval is considered. The minutes, when approved by the board of education, shall be the official records of the proceedings at which they were taken. The president and secretary shall affix their signatures to the minutes after they have been approved by the board of education. The minutes shall be kept forever as permanent public records of this board. No minutes shall be taken of the proceedings of the board of education while convened in executive session.

Electric Recordings of Board Proceedings

Where practicable, all meetings of the board of education shall be recorded in their entirety by an electrically actuated recording device. Such recordings as are made shall be considered unofficial public records of the proceedings of the board of education designed primarily to assist in the preparation of the minutes, and may be erased or destroyed three calendar years after such recordings are made.

Preservation of Written Communications to Board

Written communications to the board of education which are considered by this board as part of the public agenda shall be kept for a period of three calendar years after receipt, following which time they may be destroyed or otherwise discarded. Written communications to the board of education which are considered by this board in private executive session may be destroyed or otherwise discarded any time after such consideration, unless the board, or any member thereof, requests that such communication be saved. Such request, unless made by a majority of the board, shall not be effective to require the keeping of such communication longer than three calendar years following receipt of the communication.

Chapter 5

DE FACTO SEGREGATION

by

AUGUST W. STEINHILBER

Head of School Law Unit, United States Office of Education; member of the Ohio Bar, the District of Columbia Bar, and admitted to the practice of law in the United States Supreme Court; and author of numerous articles on school law.

Chapter 5

DE FACTO SEGREGATION

§ 5.1 Introduction

Education has found itself in the center of the battleground on two national issues—church-state and civil rights. Litigation in recent years involving school districts in civil rights cases has, however, far exceeded school litigation on any other single subject. Many school boards have found, to their amazement, that they have been named defendants in a civil rights law suit or have found the community they serve sharply divided on civil rights policy questions. The newest development in the litigation or controversy on civil rights concerns the phenomenon principally found in the North and West—de facto segregation. No review of this issue, which follows, can be adequately described without defining the subject itself.

"This article was written by August W. Steinhilber in his private capacity and no official support or endorsement by the Office of Education is intended, or should be inferred."

§ 5.2 Definition

De facto segregation can be defined as racial concentrations in the public schools caused by other than "the sanction of law" declared unconstitutional by the United States Supreme Court in the *Brown* decision.[1] Rather, these racial concentrations (also called racial imbalances) are caused by sociological and economic factors which result in housing patterns wherein nearly all Negroes live in a definite area, and Negro students attend the neighborhood school designated by school officials according to attendance zones. If racial concentrations in the school are *caused or continued* by the decisions of school officials, made in all good faith without any attempt to racially segregate, de facto segregation exists. If, however, the racial concentrations are *caused or continued* by official action with the intent to separate races by such means as gerrymandering the attendance zones (or a refusal to change an attendance zone which no longer has an educational function and is known to continue segregation), the resulting segregation is no longer de facto but de jure (i.e., by operation of law) and falls within the prohibitions handed down by the United States Supreme Court in the *Brown* decision.

§ 5.3 The issue

The conflict over de facto segregation stems from two seemingly unrelated forces, which on the racial issue find themselves going in diametrically opposite directions. Individuals and groups striving for civil liberty have proved that segregated education is inferior education, which tends to have a tremendous sociological and psychological effect on children. Thus, under this viewpoint, racial segregation, regardless of cause, is to be fought. On the other hand, many school administrators and other persons, both those within

---

[1] Brown v. Board of Education, 347 US 483, 98 LEd 873, 74 SCt 686 (1954); 349 US 294, 99 LEd 1083, 75 SCt 753 (1955).

the education profession and those interested in public education, support the concept of the "neighborhood school." This school, centrally located, is to be a school to help the community where it is physically located. Not only does this concept permit ease of administrative operation in such terms as minimum transportation and safety problems, but it promotes community affiliation and support of "their public school."

Problems arise when the community consists entirely of persons of one race and the neighborhood school concept is enforced. The problems are magnified in some school districts where school attendance zones are strictly enforced with no right of transfer available to students.

§ 5.4 Segregation and the United States Supreme Court

Since the United States Federal Government is a government of enumerated powers, and the control of education is not enumerated in the Constitution, the Supreme Court can only render a decision affecting public education if the court finds a federal interest or right which must be preserved.

Most of the United States Supreme Court rulings on racial discrimination in the public schools have been based on "the equal protection clause" of the Fourteenth Amendment to the United States Constitution.[2] This clause, interpreted loosely, means that persons must be treated alike, permitting, however, reasonable classification and distinctions.

It must be noted that this clause forbids discriminatory "state action." Discrimination by an individual in his personal capacity is not forbidden; however, he cannot act under "color of law" or use the law as a tool to enforce his discriminatory actions.[3] Some public school officials have

---

[2] "No state shall . . . deny to any person within its jurisdiction the equal protection of the laws."

[3] Ex parte Virginia, 100 US 339 (1880); Screws v. United States, 325 US 91, 89 LEd 1495, 65 SCt 1031 (1945).

mistakenly believed that state action under the Fourteenth Amendment refers to legislation, decisions, or policies of the state government. This is not the case! The United States Constitution recognizes but two levels of government within the United States—federal and state. Actions of public school officials at the local school system level, like those of any official of the state, municipal, or local government, fall within the state action category. (Please note that jurisdiction is broader than forbidding discriminatory legislation. The term "law" when referring to color of law has a much broader meaning.) Discrimination can take many forms, from an affirmative act on the part of public officials to the failing to act when duty to do so was present.

The landmark United States Supreme Court case declaring discrimination on the basis of race unconstitutional is, of course, the famous *Brown* case of 1954. In that case, the laws of Kansas, South Carolina, Virginia, and Delaware, which required segregation in the public schools based on race, were held to be in violation of the United States Constitution. The opinion contains some broad language which may be controlling in de facto segregation situations. The word "may" is used because the United States Supreme Court has *not* ruled on the constitutionality of de facto segregation. Although several cases were submitted to the high court, the Court has refused to review the decision being appealed. Chief Justice Warren, speaking for a unanimous Court, said in *Brown:*

> Today, education is perhaps the most important function of state and local governments. Compulsory school attendance laws and the great expenditures for education both demonstrate our recognition of the importance of education to our democratic society. It is required in the performance of our most basic public responsibilities, even service in the armed forces. It is the very foundation of good citizenship. Today it is a principal instrument in awakening the child to cultur-

> al values, in preparing him for later professional training, and in helping him to adjust normally to his environment. In these days, it is doubtful that any child may reasonably be expected to succeed in life if he is denied the opportunity of an education. Such an opportunity, where the state has undertaken to provide it, is a right which must be made available to all on equal terms.[4]
>
> * * *
>
> . . . Separate educational facilities are inherently unequal.[5]
>
> * * *
>
> The fundamental principle [is] that racial discrimination in public education is unconstitutional. . . . All provisions of federal, state or local law requiring or permitting such discrimination must yield to this principle.[6]

It has been argued that the term de facto segregation is a misnomer. Racial concentrations in many instances have not just happened; they were caused by action of state or local law, by legally enforced restrictive convenants in housing, and thus fall squarely within the ruling of the *Brown* decision. This line of reasoning has not to date been accepted by the Supreme Court.[6a] In fact, there is language in the *Brown* decision which apparently supports the use of neighborhood attendance areas.

In the de facto segregation cases which the Supreme Court has refused to review or, to use the technical termi-

---

[4] Brown v. Board of Education, 347 US 483, 493, 98 LEd 873, 74 SCt 686, 691 (1954).

[5] Id, 347 US 483, 495.

[6] Brown v. Board of Education, 349 US 294, 298, 99 LEd 1083, 75 SCt 753 (1955).

[6a] For a lower court ruling refusing to consider evidence of segregation in public housing in an action brought against a school district, see Deal v. Cincinnati Board of Education, 244 FSupp 572 (1965).

nology, refused to grant certiorari, several suits were brought by Negroes to force integration.[7] When the lower courts upheld the school board the Supreme Court was asked to review the decisions. In another case[8] white parents sought to enjoin the forced integration instituted by the school board, on the grounds that the United States Constitution is "color blind" and any determination based on race, even if it is to assure integration, is unconstitutional. The lower courts upheld the board's action in this case also. The denial of certiorari has no substantive legal value and no generalizations can be made from these denials.

§ 5.5 Lower federal court interpretations

Rarely, when discontinuance of racial segregation is sought, are suits based entirely upon the allegation that a racial imbalance exists. Complainants normally make a number of accusations, the first usually being that there was actual, conscious discrimination in the form of gerrymandering attendance areas, of placing all of the poorer teachers in the Negro schools, of having inadequate school plants for Negroes, of failing to give the same financial support to Negro schools, or of perpetrating other obvious acts of discrimination. The purpose, of course, is to prove the existence of de jure segregation, which is controlled by the rulin the *Brown* case. The Gary, Indiana, complaint[9] is typical of the multiple accusations. In that case the plaintiffs claimed:

1. The defendant, by assigning plaintiffs and the other members of the class to certain schools, by creat-

---

[7] Bell v. School City of Gary, Indiana, cert. den., 377 US 924, 84 SCt 1221 (1964); Downs v. Board of Education, 336 F(2d) 988 (10th Cir., 1964), cert. den., 380 US 914, 85 SCt 898 (1965).

[8] Balaban v. Rubin, 242 NYS(2d) 973 (1963); 243 NYS(2d) 472 (1963); 248 NYS(2d) 574 (1964); 250 NYS(2d) 281 (1964); cert. den. October 19, 1964.

[9] Bell v. School City (Ind), 213 FSupp 819 (1963), 324 F(2d) 209, cert. den., 377 US 924, 84 SCt 1221 (1964).

ing attendance zones, by controlling transfers from school to school, by controlling assignments from elementary to secondary schools and by the pattern of building new schools and enlarging others, maintain the Gary schools as a racially segregated school system in violation of the plaintiffs' constitutional right;

2. The defendant is discriminating against the plaintiffs and the class they represent by providing inferior facilities in all respects, including, but not limited to, overcrowded and larger classes and unequal recreational and extracurricular facilities in violation of their constitutional rights; and

3. The plaintiffs and other members of the class have a constitutional right to attend racially integrated schools and the defendant has a constitutional duty to provide and maintain a racially integrated school system.

Even when the facts of a case show that no conscious discrimination exists, the argument against de facto segregation continues on the grounds:

1. Separate facilities are inherently unequal;

2. Negro children suffer psychological harm: they are separated as if inferior; this experience is humiliating; it damages their self-confidence and their motivation;

3. The separation of races reinforces the racial prejudices of children in both white and Negro schools;

4. All children are denied the advantages of an integrated education wherein the mixing of races can bring about an understanding of different social or ethnic orders.

The New Rochelle case,[10] often mistakenly cited as

[10] Taylor v. Board of Education (NY), 191 FSupp 181 (1961), appeal dismissed 288 F(2d) 600, 195 FSupp 231, aff'd. 294 F(2d) 36, stay denied 82 SCt 10, cert. den. 82 SCt 382.

the first de facto segregation case, was decided on the factual grounds that the attendance zones had at one time been intentionally gerrymandered to exclude Negro students. Although this discriminatory act was not the action of the current board, the current board was ordered to submit a desegregation plan to the United States District Court. In this case, the court on a number of instances approached holding de facto segregation unconstitutional regardless of the case, but it did not have to reach this conclusion when de jure segregation was found present.

The first federal court to rule on the constitutionality of de facto segregation was the United States District Court for the Northern District of Indiana in the case of *Bell* v. *School City of Gary, Indiana.*[11] The federal judge reviewed the constitutional issues and the administrative problems in Gary and concluded:

> The neighborhood school which serves the students within a prescribed district is a long and well established institution in American public school education. It is almost universally used, particularly in the larger school systems It has many social, cultural and administrative advantages which are apparent without enumeration. With the use of the neighborhood school districts in any school system with a large and expanding percentage of Negro population, it is almost inevitable that a racial imbalance will result in certain schools. Nevertheless, I have seen nothing in the many cases dealing with the segregation problem which leads me to believe that the law requires that a school system developed on the neighborhood school plan, honestly and conscientiously constructed with no intention or purpose to segregate the races, must be destroyed or abandoned because the resulting effect is to have a racial imbalance in certain schools where the district

[11] 213 FSupp 819 (1963), 324 F(2d) 209, cert. den. 377 US 924 (1964).

is populated almost entirely by Negroes or whites. . . .[12]

Not only did the opinion uphold the constitutionality of de facto segregation but it cast grave doubts about any compulsory mixing of races:

> Furthermore, requiring certain students to leave their neighborhood and friends and be transferred to another school miles away, while other students, similarly situated, remained in the neighborhood school, simply for the purpose of balancing the races in the various schools, would in my opinion be indeed a violation of the equal protection clause of the Fourteenth Amendment.[13]

The United States Court of Appeals for the Seventh Circuit affirmed this decision, agreeing with the defendants:[14]

> . . . there is no affirmative U. S. Constitutional duty to change innocently arrived at school attendance districts by the mere fact that shifts in population either increase or decrease the percentage of either Negro or white pupils.

The court went further to adopt a passage of another federal court ruling: "The Constitution, in other words, does not require integration. It merely forbids discrimination." The United States Supreme Court denied certiorari in this case.

Since the *Bell* (Gary, Indiana) case, several other federal courts have ruled on de facto segregation. In the case of *Blocker* v. *The Board of Education,* a United States Dis-

[12] 213 FSupp 819, 829 (1963).

[13] Id., p. 831.

[14] Bell v. School City, 324 F(2d) 209, 213 (7th Cir., 1963); for another U.S. District Court case from the Seventh Circuit, see Webb v. Board of Education (Ill), 223 FSupp 466 (1963). The holding is, of course, the same as in the Bell case.

trict Court ordered the school district to submit a desegregation plan.[15]

It noted that this case went beyond racial imbalance, for 100% of the Negro elementary school children were in one school, separate from 99.2% of all white elementary school children. The court held that this situation approximated closely the total separation condemned in *Brown*. It declined to decide whether the segregation was de jure or de facto:

> . . . can it be said that one type of segregation, having its basis in state law or evasive schemes to defeat desegregation is to be proscribed, while another having the same effect but another cause, is to be condoned? Surely, the Constitution is made of sturdier stuff.[16]

The court implied that the attendance areas in existence could not now be drawn and justified by normal criteria supporting the neighborhood school policy, for the Negro attendance area was obviously unreasonable, being disproportionately small and resulting in a small student body which was 99% Negro. Superimposed on the attendance zones was a strict "no transfer" policy. It should be noted that the board had been aware of the nature of the attendance zones and the results for some time and had done nothing.

In requiring that the school board submit a desegregation plan, the court stressed that the current legal philosophy that the Fourteenth Amendment only forbids discrimination but does not require integration, has not been adopted by the United States Supreme Court. Rather, this doctrine has been developed by lesser United States courts with which the court in this case disagreed.

The limitations of the scope of the decision were carefully noted. First, the neighborhood school policy is not uncon-

---

[15] (NY), 226 FSupp 208 (1964).

[16] Id., p. 223.

stitutional but likewise, it is not immutable. Next, racial imbalance and segregation are not synonymous, and racial imbalance not tantamount to segregation is not necessarily unconstitutional.

The decision noted that other cases having opposite rulings, like the *Bell* case,[17] were cases involving racial imbalance, not total segregation, and that the Constitution does *not* require proportionate representation of white and Negro children in each elementary school.

When the desegregation plan was filed, the court clarified its ruling by saying the compulsory distribution of races to receive proportional representation was not required.[18] The purpose of the decision was to discontinue 100% segregation. The school board accepted the decision and decided not to appeal.[19]

The neighborhood school concept was specifically attacked in a case involving an Ohio school district.[20] The judge quoted the Supreme Court in the *Brown* decision that "revision of school districts and attendance areas into compact units to achieve a system of determining admission to the public schools on a nonracial basis"[21] was a factor which could be used in implementing the *Brown* decision. He concluded the court did not order integration but ordered an end to segregation, and such end could be accomplished by consolidating a school district into attendance units. The court went on in ruling for the school board and noted that the plaintiffs were requesting action forbidden by the Constitution, in ordering pupils admitted to a school because of their race. Specifically, the court said:

---

17 Bell v. School City (Ind), 213 FSupp 819, 324 F(2d) 208 (1963).

18 Blocker v. Board of Education (NY), 229 FSupp 709 (1964).

19 For information on the right of other parents and taxpayers to intervene, see Blocker v. Board of Education (NY), 229 FSupp 714 (1964).

20 Lynch v. Kenston School Dist. Board of Education (Ohio), 229 FSupp 740 (1964).

21 Brown v. Board of Education, 349 US 294, 300, 99 LEd 1083, 75 SCt 753 (1955).

> The law is color-blind and, in cases such as this, that principle, which was designed to insure equal protection to all citizens, is both a shield and a sword. While protecting them in their right to be free from racial discrimination, it at the same time denies them the right to consideration on a racial basis where there has been no discrimination.

This court recognized that to some extent this decision was in conflict with the decision in the *Blocker* case, but concluded that the *Blocker* decision was erroneous and its precedent would not be followed.

In another case,[22] decided by the same court as the *Lynch* case just reviewed, the construction of several elementary schools was attacked on the grounds that the children who would attend these schools would be predominantly Negro. The Negro plaintiff emphasized that this was not a case like the *Bell* (Gary, Indiana) case, since the school board had knowledge that this result would occur from the building of these schools. The court found no intentional wrongdoing and refused to stop the construction, saying:

> Recognition of the problem of racial imbalance, caused through no fault of the board does not mean the board has an affirmative duty to relieve the problem. (at p. 387)

The litigation involving Kansas City, Kansas,[23] was unique, in that before 1954 a de jure segregated educational system was maintained. After the *Brown* decision a policy was initiated to integrate "as rapidly as classroom space provided." Under this policy attendance areas were set up wherein, with rare exceptions, each child lived within 1.5 miles from the school he attended. Because of ur-

---

[22] Craggett v. Board of Education (Ohio), 234 FSupp 381 (1964). Accord: Deal v. Cincinnati Board of Education, 244 FSupp 572 (1965).

[23] Downs v. Board of Education, 336 F(2d) 988 (10th Cir., 1964).

ban renewal projects, the racial complexion of several attendance areas became Negro. The court agreed with the plaintiffs that a racial imbalance existed in the public schools and that the school district could not use "the neighborhood school system as a guise for the purpose of perpetuating racial segregation." The court concluded, however, that the school authorities had acted in good faith, and there was no evidence of intentional gerrymandering. Turning to the question of whether there was an affirmative duty to eliminate de facto segregation, the court held "no":

> While there seems to be authority to support that contention [of an affirmative duty], the rule is that although the Fourteenth Amendment prohibits segregation, it does not command integration of the races in the public schools, and Negro children have no constitutional right to have white children attend school with them.

One court[24] specifically has ruled that such an affirmative duty does exist. In this case, no deliberate intention to segregate the races was proven and it was established that attendance lines were drawn for valid reasons. The court went on, however, to say that under the circumstances in that community that "a nonwhite attendance of appreciably more than fifty percent in any one school is tantamount to segregation." The court accepted expert testimony that racially imbalanced schools were not conducive to learning. Thus the real issue was whether there was a constitutional duty to provide equal educational opportunities for all children within the system.

The judge found such a duty, and specifically rejected the *Bell* (Gary, Indiana) decision and the legal philosophy that the Constitution does not require integration but merely forbids discrimination. The language of this case is in-

---

[24] Barksdale v. Springfield School Committee (Mass), 237 FSupp 543 (1965).

teresting in the way the obligation is placed on public education:

> Education is tax supported and compulsory, and public school educators, therefore, *must deal with inadequacies* within the education system as they arise, and it matters not that the inadequacies are not of their making. (at p. 546) (Emphasis added)

This statement has implications far beyond the confines of de facto segregation. On appeal the decision was vacated and the case dismissed.[24a] Although the court of appeals rejected any language in the prior ruling that a constitutional duty exists to desegregate the schools, the reversal was not based on the merits of the case. The court determined that prior to litigation the school district had resolved to eliminate racial concentrations and that the law suit was premature. No final ruling was made on the right to equal educational opportunities, but the court noted that if the defendants disregard their previously announced plan, a new action may be brought and appropriate relief, if any, will be determined at that time.

§ 5.6 State cases and state law

Basically this chapter is focused upon de facto segregation and the United States Constitution. A school district should, however, determine if there are any state laws or state administrative regulations which are specifically applicable; for if such exist, the litigation may be in a state court with state law at issue.

The state of New Jersey offers a fine example of this difference. While, as has been pointed out, the applicability of the United States Constitution to de facto segregation has not been clarified, there is little doubt extreme racial imbalances must be corrected under New Jersey law. The state constitution says in part, Article 1, section 5:

[24a] Springfield School Committee v. Barksdale, 348 F(2d) 261 (1st Cir., 1965).

> No person shall be denied the enjoyment of any civil or military right, nor be discriminated against in the exercise of any civil or military right, nor be segregated in the militia or in the public schools, because of religious principles, race, color, ancestry or national origin.

The state law provides in New Jersey Statutes Annotated, 18:11-1:

> Each school district shall provide suitable school facilities and accommodations for all children who reside in the district and desire to attend the public schools therein. Such facilities and accommodations shall include proper school buildings, together with furniture and equipment, convenience of access thereto, and courses of study suited to the ages and attainments of all pupils between the ages of five and twenty years. Such facilities and accommodations may be provided either in schools within the district convenient of access to the pupils, or as provided in sections 18:14-5 to 18:14-9 of this title.

The commissioner of education[25] has on a number of occasions found "an extreme racial imbalance" and has ruled this constitutes under New Jersey law a deprivation of educational opportunity and has ordered the school district to file a desegregation plan.

The action of the commissioner of education in ordering a district to file a desegregation plan and the provisions of subsequent plan were attacked in a court action.[26] In this case the plaintiffs, parents of white children, brought an action to stop the desegregation plan, on the grounds that the plan was adopted solely because of racial considerations

---

[25] Fischer v. Board of Education of Orange, New Jersey, May 16, 1963; Booker v. Board of Education of City of Plainfield, New Jersey, June 26, 1963; Spruil v. Board of Education of Englewood, New Jersey, July 1, 1963.

[26] Fuller v. Volk (NJ), 230 FSupp 25 (1964).

and that it discriminated against white children solely because of their color. The issue thus drawn was not whether there was a constitutional duty to act where de facto segregation exists but whether the board was prohibited from acting. The federal court ruled it was not so prohibited. It also noted that there was no evidence that racial integration discriminates against white persons, nor were any of the provisions of the plan an infringement of their constitutional rights.

Several state courts have had to rule on a different de facto question: Can the fact that a child is assigned to a de facto segregated school be used as a defense against complying with the compulsory attendance laws? In a recent ruling a New Jersey court held that the fact that a child was assigned to a racially segregated school was no defense to a prosecution for violation of the attendance laws.[27] It is important to mention that this court recognized that there were more appropriate means available in New Jersey to correct any illegal segregation. An earlier New York case, however, reasoned: "Parents have a constitutionally guaranteed right to elect no education for their children rather than subject them to discriminatory inferior education.[28]"

§ 5.7 Generalizations made from court rulings

After reviewing these decisions, several legal generalizations can be made:

1. Most federal courts have found no affirmative duty on the part of school districts to modify attendance zones honestly drawn.

2. The existence of an all-Negro school does not necessarily mean discrimination exists, but the burden of proving discrimination is upon the plaintiff.

---

[27] State v. Vaughn, 44 NJ 142, 207 A(2d) 537 (1965).

[28] In re Skipwith, 180 NYS(2d) 852, 14 Misc(2d) 325 (1958); see also Dobbins v. Commonwealth, 198 Va 697, 96 SE(2d) 154 (1957).

3. Although the United States Constitution is said to be "color blind," this does not mean racial factors must be ignored when drawing attendance lines. It is also true that the question of race cannot be used to the advantage of minority groups and the disadvantage of others.

4. The neighborhood school concept is not of itself either constitutional or unconstitutional, but can be used either in a constitutional or unconstitutional manner.

5. Compulsory attendance laws may or may not be enforceable against children in inferior Negro schools.

6. State laws may require school districts to take affirmative action, and such laws are not unconstitutional.

§ 5.8 The United States Civil Rights Act of 1964

Title IV of the Civil Rights Act (Public Law 88-352) authorized the commissioner of education to provide technical assistance and financial aid to assist in solving problems dealing with desegregation, and authorizes the attorney general in interstate suits to require desegregation. The title, however, specifies that desegregation "shall not mean assignment of students to public schools in order to overcome racial imbalance" (sec. 401(b)), and that

> nothing herein shall empower any official or court of the United States to issue any order seeking to achieve a racial balance in any school by requiring the transportation of pupils or students from one school to another or one school district to another in order to achieve racial balance, or otherwise enlarge existing power of the court to insure compliance with constitutional standards. (sec. 407 (a) (2)).

Furthermore, section 410 provides that any classification and assignment for reasons other than race, color, religion, or national origin are not forbidden. It thus appears the neighborhood school and use of attendance zones are not forbidden if they are not used to discriminate.

Title VI of the same law forbids discrimination in any federally assisted program which, of course, includes all school districts receiving federal funds. Discrimination is further defined in the regulations controlling the operation of Title VI. (See Title 45, Code of Federal Regulations, sec. 80.3). The law and regulations promulgated under the law specify that no person shall, on the ground of race, color, or national origin, be subject to discrimination under any program receiving federal financial assistance. No reference is made to de facto segregation or racial imbalances.

The use of attendance zones as an acceptable means of compliance with Title VI was spelled out in the Office of Education's "General Statement of Policies under Title VI of the Civil Rights Act of 1964 Respecting Desegregation of Elementary and Secondary Schools." Racially separate zones are forbidden and new racial zones can be drawn if they follow natural boundaries or perimeters of compact areas surrounding particular schools. Initial assignments of a pupil shall be to the school in his zone. Furthermore, a child has a right to attend the school in his attendance zone, and transfer outside of an attendance area shall not take into consideration race, color, or national origin.

As shown, the Civil Rights Act does not outlaw de facto segregation as such, but it certainly covers de jure segregation, regardless of where it occurs and of whatever means are used to discriminate, including the use of attendance zones.

§ 5.9 Corrective action

De facto segregation exists and regardless of its cause it may produce a profound effect upon a school district. This would not be the first social ill a school district has had to face, nor will it be the last. This ill, however, has direct educational implications, for there is sound educational evidence that most, if not all, of the schools in these areas of minority racial concentration are not of the same quality as schools in other areas. What can the school or school board do to correct the situation? Because of basic community differences, psychological and political, no one single answer can solve the problem for all communities. Although what may work in one area may fail elsewhere, the following are approaches which have been used by some communities, and they may suggest a possible approach:

1. Open enrollment policy. This plan seeks to mitigate the strict adherence to attendance zone, which often is a primary factor in continuing de facto segregation. The open enrollment policy, also called free choice plan, permits each child, as a matter of right, to attend the school nearest his home. Children may, however, request transfers to other schools on a first-come, first-served basis as long as space is available. If transportation is not also provided the plan may not work, because the parent in a slum area may not be able to pay to have his child transported to a school of his choice. Another disadvantage of this plan is that the initiative is on the parents and children to make decisions and then to request action by school officials. The areas where the educational problems caused by de facto segregation are most acute are also areas where individual parents are least likely to make such decisions and requests.

2. Rezoning of present attendance zones. This system is as simple to describe as its name indicates, but its implementation may not be that easy. Areas of minority racial concentration are known and these are subdivided in such a manner as to transfer some of the children to other schools. This plan may not work where the racial concentration covers a large area.

3. Princeton plan. This plan involves the restructuring of the current grade structure and can best be described by illustration. Suppose a school district had two elementary schools, grades 1 to 6, of equal size, one being all white, the other all Negro. The grade structure would be changed so that all children of grades 1, 2, and 3 would attend one

school and all children of grades 4, 5, and 6 would attend the other.

4. Enlarge attendance zones. This plan is especially suited for a district having many small schools. Certain small schools could be abandoned or used for administrative offices, and larger school buildings which would service a larger area, with a more cosmopolitan base for enrollment, could be built.

5. Use of new site selections. New sites can be selected on the border of minority racial concentration, and the attendance area drawn to include part of the territory of this concentration and part outside. If used, a drawback of this plan is that the problem of replacing outdated or deficient schools in the heart of residential areas of a homogeneous ethnic population may not be met.

6. Busing. The most controversial, and in many ways the least effective, means of correcting de facto segregation and maintaining community support consists of transporting children from schools where racial concentration exists to other schools, and at the same time transporting children from these "other" schools to schools of minority racial concentrations. To be sure, this method insures the mixing of races, but may involve the loss of community allegiance to their community schools. Another disadvantage is that when a pupil is enrolled outside of his neighborhood, his teacher may have less access to the parent, thus weakening the educational ties between home and school.

7. Establish educational park. The establishment of a central educational park or parks composed of elementary, junior high, and senior high schools, or any other organizational plan of a K-12 system, has been proposed. Such an establishment may be considered if extensive building is contemplated. Such a plan necessitates a tremendous acreage in order to include the many building facilities to carry out the educational design. Thousands of pupils would have to be transported to the educational park. Many existing

schools would be either torn down because of obsolescence, used for other purposes, or become a capital loss. Although there is merit to such a plan, it cannot solve the problem unless there is a mixture of individuals with different socio-economic backgrounds. In the large metropolitan cities, the extent of segregated areas, of various kinds, is so extensive that it may be near to impossible to achieve the socio-economic balance that many believe is necessary to solve the problems caused by de facto segregation.

§ 5.10 Compensatory education

There are school districts where the number of persons in a de facto segregated area and/or the size of the area is so large that any plan to change attendance zones for the purpose of correcting a de facto segregation situation will fail. What can be done with the educational problems in an area, as in New York City, where the white enrollment in public schools has dropped from 68% to 53% from 1957 to 1964? During that same period the percentage of Negro pupils has risen 53% and of Puerto Rican pupils 38%. The trend in the white population has been to move out of New York City or to send their children to private schools. In large areas of the city there are no white public school pupils. One answer appears to be "compensatory education." By this it is meant special educational programs to supplement current programs. These could include reading improvement programs, special counseling, prekindergarten programs, special programs to bring parents into the school setting, special honors or monetary rewards for teachers in these schools, special in-service training for teachers, to mention a few. The content or scope of compensatory education is, of course, determined by the local school board, which understands the problems of its community.

§ 5.11 Administrative problems

Many problems can arise in the preparation and implementation of a plan to integrate de facto segregated schools or to correct racial imbalances in the schools. Although the scope of these problems cannot be forecast, a wise school system should not be caught unawares. The following are examples of such problems:

A. Initial preparation and planning

1. Studies.

   a. In anticipation of objections and problems, and to satisfy them, should studies be made of levels of educational achievement among students?

   b. Should public opinion, student opinion, or teacher opinion polls be taken to assess possible objections and problems?

2. Publicity.

   a. Is advance notice of planned desegregation desirable (e.g., can it be expected to inspire "outside agitators?")

   b. How can a school district organize the support of the press? of civic groups, churches, and other organizations?

3. Problems to anticipate.

   a. Would integration lead to an exodus to the suburbs? to increased enrollment in private schools?

   b. Upon redistribution of pupils from schools which meet special neighborhood needs through particularized course offerings (e.g., language courses in Hebrew, Italian, Polish), what arrangements can be made to continue to meet these needs for students who—after integration—are no longer concentrated in the neighborhood schools?

   c. Should disciplinary policies be modified and explained to meet behavior problems of a type or scale unfamiliar to supervisors and teachers? Should they be altered or planned to avoid sensitive situations, where teacher and student are of different races?

d. Are special textbooks or courses desirable to (1) more adequately meet the needs of students from other than the "middle class," toward which many textbooks are oriented? (2) to integrate a study of "human relations" into the materials used in other courses?

e. What methods might be available to prepare community, parents, and students for integrated teaching staffs?

B. Acceptance by parents and community

1. How do school officials enlist the support of community members who may be sympathetic to integration? (Note: In many instances acceptance of integration has been found to be positively correlated with amount of education.)

2. If general publicity is used, how do you avoid alienation of individuals and groups who might otherwise be enlisted if they were approached with publicity specifically oriented toward their attitudes and circumstances?

3. Are special efforts desirable to enlist the support of parents of minority group children, who are not ordinarily active in civic affairs?

C. Acceptance by teachers and school supervisory personnel

1. How can an exodus of teachers from newly-integrated schools be prevented? by salesmanship? mandatory assignment? incentive pay?

2. Should teacher training methods be modified to prepare teachers for the difficulties of teaching,

in a single class, children of different racial backgrounds, social classes, levels of achievement? What methods might be effective? Should new courses or course content be introduced or altered in teacher training institutions? In in-service training? Should practice teaching be required in "problem" schools?

3. How can teachers be aided to overcome biases or fears concerning the teaching of students of other ethnic backgrounds?
4. What special arrangements might be made to lessen the burden on the teacher of educationally retarded students?—smaller classes? supplementary training for the disadvantaged student in the summer or at night?
5. What might be done to utilize teachers from "disadvantaged" schools, who may not meet the higher standards possibly demanded in the integrated schools?
6. Where integration of supervisory staffs takes place, is any special preparation necessary before introducing supervisory personnel who are members of minority ethnic groups?
7. Should service in "problem" schools or integrated schools be a prerequisite to certification for higher supervisory positions?

D. Acceptance by students

1. By students in the minority group
   a. Will substandard educational background, fear of the difficulties of social adjustment, or fear of higher standards at integrated schools deter minority-group students from electing to transfer when "open enrollment" is offered them?

2. By majority and minority
   a. Should matter be introduced into the curriculum, or by some other means, to prepare students for the problems which might be anticipated in integrated situations?
   b. Should students participate, through seminars or student government, in the planning for integration, to increase possibility of acceptance of integration?
   c. Would gradual integration make total integration more practicable? less practicable?
   d. Should teaching staffs be integrated first in order to prepare students for integration of student body, or should student body be integrated first to prepare for integration of the staff?

E. Integration of "low achievement" students

1. How can the student who is educationally retarded be integrated without debasing the quality of education in the system or affecting it adversely?
2. How can the student attempt to raise his achievement level?—by intensive instruction? summer classes? smaller classes? increased counseling and psychiatric and social services?
3. What can be done to meet the problem of teaching children to read whose parents do not read? What about adult education to encourage parents' reading? parent-teacher contacts to attempt to gain parental support by explaining the objects and importance of education? (Note: The success in some New York City neighborhoods of encouraging Spanish-speaking parents to take active and leadership roles in P.T.A. was accom-

plished by contacting them through Spanish-speaking school representatives.)

4. Will ability grouping become a sophisticated method of segregation within integrated schools?

§ 5.12 Conclusion

As indicated in this chapter, de facto segregation and the opposing social and political forces using this issue as a battleground have raised many problems, both in terms of knotty legal questions as well as serious policy and administrative questions. The problems are not localized in a few communities; the geographic area where de facto segregation exists is immense. In 1960 nearly two thirds of all Negroes in the North lived in eighteen cities, and statistics gathered by the Housing and Home Finance Agency indicate racial concentrations exist in southern cities to nearly the same extent as in the North. As is true with most problems of this complexity and magnitude, there are no easy conclusions or solutions.

The law is unsettled and thus subject to change. New laws or rulings may occur at either state or national level. For example, the Massachusetts legislature enacted a law on August 18, 1965, which states in part:

> Section 37C. It is hereby declared to be the policy of the commonwealth to encourage all school committees to adopt as educational objectives the promotion of racial balance and the correction of existing racial imbalance in the public schools. The prevention or elimination of racial imbalance shall be an objective in all decisions involving the drawing or altering of school attendance lines and the selection of new school sites.
>
> Section 37D. The school committee of each city, town and district shall, annually, at such time and in such form as the commissioner shall determine, submit statistics sufficient to enable a determination to be made

> of the percent of nonwhite pupils in all public schools and in each school under the jurisdiction of each such committee. Whenever the state board of education finds that racial imbalance exists in a public school it shall notify in writing the school committee or regional school district committee having jurisdiction over such school that such finding has been made. The school committee shall thereupon prepare a plan to eliminate such racial imbalance and file a copy of such plan with the board. The term "racial imbalance" refers to a ratio between nonwhite and other students in public schools which is sharply out of balance with the racial composition of the society in which nonwhite children study, serve and work. For the purpose of this section, racial imbalance shall be deemed to exist when the percent of nonwhite students in any public school is in excess of fifty percent of the total number of students in such school. . . .

There can, therefore, be no legal conclusions other than the generalizations made earlier in this chapter.

Although there are no assured solutions to the administrative and political problems which can be listed in textbook manner, in many respects these problems are not of any greater severity than others currently faced in public education. One need only to look at some of the difficulties encountered and solved in dual enrollment (shared time) programs, team teaching, regional educational agreements, professional negotiations and educational T.V., to name a few. There is no reason to believe that de facto segregation cannot likewise be successfully handled.

As for the statement made by some that de facto segregation was by definition not caused by school authorities and thus there is no educational obligation, the answer is simply that this causation criteria was never a deterrent in facing other educational needs. Schools have long assisted in solving educational problems not of their making. As I heard one educator say, "We didn't cause children to be born or become blind, but we have met the educational challenge with these children as with many more who have some physical or mental handicaps."

Chapter 6

PUBLIC EMPLOYEE NEGOTIATING AND SCHOOL BOARD AUTHORITY

by

REYNOLDS C. SEITZ

Dean and Professor of Law, September 1953-1965 (Professor of Law to present), Marquette University Law School, Milwaukee, Wisconsin; specialist in labor, constitutional, and school law; experienced labor arbitrator on panels of American Arbitration Association, Federal Mediation and Conciliation Service and Wisconsin Employment Relations Board; member Committee on Government Employee Relations of Labor Law Section of American Bar Association; member National Academy of Arbitrators; formerly assistant to the superintendent of public schools in Omaha and St. Louis; senior attorney, National Labor Relations Board, Washington, D.C.; labor relations attorney, Montgomery Ward and Co., Chicago; executive, Chicago Daily News; associate professor, Northwestern University; editor of volume Law and the School Principal; editor in chief, NOLPE School Law Newsletter; and frequent writer and lecturer on school law.

Chapter 6

PUBLIC EMPLOYEE NEGOTIATING AND SCHOOL BOARD AUTHORITY

§ 6.1 Introduction

The title of this chapter might more specifically have been "Legality of Efforts of Public School Personnel to

Join Employee Organizations and to Bargain Collectively and Exercise Concerted Pressure to Attain Employment Goals." Such a title would have been too cumbersome for printing and, furthermore, the title as set forth probably better focuses attention upon the major concern on the part of many who contemplate the efforts being made by public employee groups to bargain collectively, relative to employment conditions.

§ 6.2 Legal connotations of collective bargaining or professional negotiations

Those who question the right of public school teachers to negotiate and bargain collectively most frequently express their basic objection in the contention that negotiation and collective bargaining constitute a serious invasion of school board authority.

To understand this objection it is vitally necessary to realize at the outset that the term "negotiations and collective bargaining" has a legal connotation much different than merely providing various groups an opportunity to appear before, or in some other fashion present their requests to a school board. School boards have permitted this type of approach for many years.

"Collective bargaining" or the fundamentally synonymous term "professional negotiations" has a legal connotation which means much more than merely permitting the school board complete discretion as to what procedure to follow in reacting to requests that may be presented to it by various groups.

In order to react to the validity of the assertion that such a concept of collective bargaining does constitute a serious invasion of school board authority, it seems necessary to delineate fully what is legally meant by collective bargaining. The concept of what constitutes good faith collective bargaining has been worked out to a large extent by the federal courts and the National Labor Relations Board in interpreting section 8 (d) of the National Labor Relations Act,[1] which by its specific language imposes a duty on employees and unions to "meet at reasonable times and confer in good faith with respect to wages, hours and other terms and conditions of employment" and goes on to state that "such obligation does not compel either party to agree to a proposal or require the making of a concession."

It is possible that if state statutory language differs from that of the National Labor Relations Act, there could be an interpretation of good faith bargaining somewhat different than the description which follows. It seems certain, however, that no state legislation calling for negotiation will require, by way of bargaining approach, more than does the National Labor Relations Act and the decisions interpreting the responsibility imposed by the Act. It is submitted that the guide lines laid down by the National Labor Relations Board and the federal courts presently give the most far reaching definition of the concept of good faith collective bargaining.

§ 6.3 Analysis of good faith bargaining

Good faith bargaining often does require, in reacting to demands that are not acceptable, the offering of reasons for rejection and some counter-proposals.[2] It requires recognition of both parties, not merely formal but real, that collective bargaining is a shared process in which each party has a right to play an active role.[3] In this area there has been a rather recent interesting development. In December, 1964, the National Labor Relations Board in the *General Electric*

[1] 29 USC, sec. 141 et seq.

[2] NLRB v. Pilling & Sons Co., 119 F(2d) 32 (3d Cir., 1941); NLRB v. Montgomery Ward & Co., 133 F(2d) 676 (9th Cir., 1943); Dierks Forests, Inc. (NLRB decision) 57 LRRM 1087, 1089 (1964).

[3] East Bay Union of Machinists, Local 1304 USW v. NLRB, 322 F(2d) 411, 415 (DC Cir., 1963).

Company[4] case dealt with what is familiarly known as the Boulwarism[5] approach.

The fact situation showed that the employer listened to and analyzed the demands and arguments supplied by the union and then made an offer to the union which included everything the employer found to be warranted. Nothing was held back for later negotiations, and the company took the position that the offer would not be changed unless new information or a significant development in facts indicated that adjustments were warranted. The company justified this position on the ground that it engages in year-around research to determine what is right for the employees, and when bargaining begins, it listens to the union as part of its overall research, and then on the basis of overall study makes an offer which includes everything it believes is warranted. The company does not actually say "take it or leave it" but does make it clear it will not change its position unless new information is presented. It made it clear it would take a strike rather than do what it considered wrong policy.

The National Labor Relations Board condemned this type of bargaining on the ground that it was tantamount to mere formality and served to transform the role of the employee-representative from a joint participant in the bargaining process to that of an adviser. In practical effect the board felt that the position of the company was akin to that of a party who entered into negotiations with a predetermined resolve not to budge from an initial position—an attitude inconsistent with good faith bargaining.[6]

In deciding the *General Electric Company* case the National Labor Relations Board also alluded to the fact that the company mounted a campaign of communications, both before and during negotiations, for the purpose of dispar-

---

4 57 LRRM 1491 (1964).

5 The name of an industrial relations executive at General Electric.

6 The General Electric Co. case has reached the federal court of appeals and is likely ultimately to go to the United States Supreme Court.

aging and discrediting the union and to seek to persuade the employees to exert pressure on the union to submit to the will of the employer. The communications were referred to as reaching "flood" proportions. The board felt this approach on the part of the employer overlooked the requirement of *National Labor Relations Board* v. *Insurance Agents Internat. Union, AFL-CIO*[7] that the statutory representative is the one with whom the employer must deal in conducting bargaining negotiations, and that he can no longer bargain directly or individually with the employees.

§ 6.4 Capitulation or discussion

Collective bargaining does not mean the necessity that the public employer must ultimately capitulate to demands.[8] It does not mean that there is a necessity to make some concessions as an outgrowth of every demand.[9] Good faith bargaining does not sanction an administrative body or a court undertaking to exercise its wisdom to determine if a particular proposal was reasonable or unreasonable.[10]

§ 6.5 Conditions of collective bargaining or professional negotiations

The United States Supreme Court,[11] in interpreting the meaning of good faith collective bargaining under the National Labor Relations Act, has recognized three categories of proposals:

1. Those that are illegal and therefore cannot be bargained about.

---

[7] 361 US 477, 484-5, 4 LEd(2d) 454, 80 SCt 419 (1960).

[8] NLRB v. American Nat. Ins. Co., 343 US 395, 96 LEd 1027, 72 SCt 824 (1952).

[9] White v. NLRB, 255 F(2d) 564 (5th Cir., 1958); NLRB v. American Aggregate Co., 335 F(2d) 253 (5th Cir., 1964).

[10] Id., at pp. 566-7; Dierks Forests, Inc., supra note 2.

[11] NLRB v. Wooster Division of Borg-Warner Corp., 356 US 342, 78 SCt 718 (1958).

2. Those that may be bargained about if the parties voluntarily wish to do so.

3. Those that are mandatory and must be bargained about.

Proposals that come within the category of wages, hours and other terms and conditions of employment fall within the mandatory area. Certainly falling within the conditions of employment would be such things as assignments during out of school hours to supervision of extracurricular events, class loads, class size, use of teacher assistants and rest periods.

It would appear that decisions on curriculum content could technically be viewed as remaining solely the prerogative of administration and the school board. In this respect, however, it would seem wise for the school board not to adopt a too literal approach. Many employer leaders in industrial relations adopt the attitude that it is not wise to be too technical about drawing the line, on the ground that the subject-matter does not fall within the mandatory area. These leaders feel that industrial peace will be best insured if the employer is willing to discuss most matters at the bargaining table. Of course, the industrial leaders that adopt this attitude realize that bargaining does not mean capitulation.

It is very significant that the United States Supreme Court recognized that a party cannot be forced to bargain on certain matters that are illegal. This principle answers objections of those who attempt to argue that public employee bargaining is blocked by statutes which may exact budget limitations, by such things as state salary laws and by state tenure, retirement and pension laws. The principle recognizes that it would be improper to ignore the problem of public employee bargaining colliding with existing statutes. This recognition, however, requires a realistic appreciation of what it means to collide with the statute. For example, even if there is a state tenure law setting forth reasons for "for cause" discharge, it would still be possible to bargain for intermediate grievance procedure.

§ 6.6 Evaluation of facts

In facing up to whether there has been good faith bargaining, it must be recognized that it is necessary to evaluate the facts. This can be difficult because it requires an objective evaluation of the parties' attitude as reflected in their course of conduct during negotiation. In this area it is significant to take account of the National Labor Relations Board language in the *General Electric Company* case.[12] The board commented that

> in challenging the trial examiner's finding . . . General Electric argues that an employer cannot be found guilty of having violated its statutory duty where it is desirous of entering into a collective bargaining agreement, where it has met and conferred with the bargaining representative on all required subjects of bargaining as prescribed by statute and has not taken unlawful unilateral action, and where it has not demanded the inclusion in the bargaining contract of any illegal clauses or insisted to an impasse upon any nonmandatory bargaining provision. In compliance with the above, General Electric further argues that an employer's technique of bargaining is not subject to approval or disapproval by the board.

To this argument the board responded:

> General Electric reads the statute requirement for bargaining collectively too narrowly . . . An employer may still have failed to discharge its statutory obligation to bargain in good faith. As the Supreme Court has said,[13] "The board is authorized to order the cessation

[12] Supra note 4 at 1499.

[13] NLRB v. Katz, 369 US 736, 747, 8 LEd(2d) 230, 82 SCt 1107 (1962).

> of behavior which is in effect a refusal to negotiate, or which directly obstructs or inhibits the actual process of discussion, or which reflects a cast of mind against reaching an agreement" . . . Good faith bargaining thus involves both a procedure for meeting and negotiating, which might be called the externals of collective bargaining, and a bona fide intention, the presence or absence of which must be discerned from the record.

In connection with this statement it is significant to note the comments of the Chairman of the National Labor Relations Board.[13a] He states:

> The decision does not hold that an employer may not after appropriate bargaining make a fair and final offer to the union representing his employees. It does not hold that an employer may not criticize union leaders or proposals. It does not hold that an employer may not communicate with his employees. Those who tell you differently do you a disservice. The board simply applied accepted principles to a unique bargaining situation.

In connection with the evaluation of good faith, certain types of conduct have been held to be sufficient of themselves to establish a lack of good faith bargaining. A refusal to discuss or provide data necessary to intelligent discussion of a subject within the mandatory area of bargaining is an example.[14] So, also, is insistence upon including in a contract a proposal that is outside the scope of mandatory bargaining.[15]

[13a] McCulloch, address delivered Oct. 28, 1965 at Annual Conference of Texas Industry, reported 60 LRRM 145.

[14] NLRB v. Truitt Mfg. Co., 351 US 149, 100 LEd 1027, 76 SCt 753 (1956); NLRB v. Item Co., 220 F(2d) 956 (5th Cir., 1955).

[15] Allen Bradley Co. and Lodge No. 78, Tool and Die Makers International Assoc., 45 LRRM 1505, 127 NLRB No. 8 (1960).

§ 6.7 Authority

It is, of course, apparent that when the school board undertakes collective bargaining, as it has been defined, it undertakes burdens which it does not need to assume if it does not bargain collectively. The assumption, however, of these burdens does not mean that the board has delegated away its authority. In this respect it is interesting to recall that the history of industrial relations establishes that when the employer was first confronted with the statutory necessity of bargaining collectively, he complained that he was being forced to delegate away his authority. The courts did not agree with him. The courts recognized that he did assume additional burdens but that he still retained ultimate authority to make final decisions.

In the public employee field, if legislative bodies decree or courts permit collective bargaining, it represents a decision, just as it did in the industrial field, that employee relations will be benefited. It does not appear that this decision can be logically frustrated by the argument that the provision results in forcing a school board to delegate away its authority.

§ 6.8 Right to organize

Now that some substance has been given to the term "collective bargaining or negotiations" it seems appropriate to approach the central topic of this chapter by presenting a very brief perspective on the history of collective bargaining in general. To be very direct about the matter, after some early struggles in which the efforts of industrial workers to join labor organizations and bargain collectively were condemned by the courts and sometimes the legislatures as illegal conspiracies and later illegal torts, the industrial worker received through legislation and judicial decision almost complete support for his effort to join labor organizations and bargain collectively. This was surely evident, at least from the middle 1930's, after the impetus given by the passage of the federal Wagner Act creating the National Labor Relations Board.

In the public employee field, the push of such employees to join employee organizations whose goals are betterment of employment conditions, has been gaining momentum since the end of World War II.

Such employees have not, however, automatically been given the same rights as industrial workers. Hurdles have been erected by judicial decisions, and in some instances by legislative attitudes.

A hurdle which exists through legislation[16] and judicial decision,[17] but which is fast disappearing in most jurisdictions, was the denial of the right to join an employee organization or union, on the ground of inconsistency with government employment. To the extent that this attitude still exists, it would seem possible to challenge it on First Amendment constitutional grounds. It is difficult to see why such outlook is not a constitutional interference with the right of freedom to assemble.

§ 6.9 Denial of the opportunity to bargain collectively

A more usual hurdle[18] today is the denial of the opportunity to bargain collectively.

The only logical justification for prohibiting public employees from joining employee organizations which have

[16] CodeofAla, tit. 55, secs. 317 (1) to 317 (4) (Supp. 1957); GaCode Ann, secs. 54-909, 54-9923 (1961); NCGenStat, secs. 95-97 to 95-100 (Supp. 1959); VaCode, secs. 40.65 to 40.67 (1950).

[17] Perez v. Board of Police Comm'rs., 78 CalApp(2d) 638, 178 P(2d) 537 (1947); People ex rel Fursman v. City of Chicago, 278 Ill 318, 116 NE 158 (1917); King v. Priest, 357 Mo 68, 206 SW(2d) 547 (1947).

[18] Mugford v. Mayor and City Council of Baltimore, 185 Md 206, 44 A(2d) 745 (1945); City of Cleveland v. Division 268, Amalgamated Assn. of Street, Elect. and Motor Coach Employees of Amer., 30 OhioOp 395 (1945); Nutter v. Santa Monica, 74 CalApp(2d) 292, 168 P(2d) 741 (1946); Springfield v. Clouse, 356 Mo 1239, 206 SW(2d) 539 (1947); Miami Water Works, Local No. 654 v. Miami, 157 Fla 445, 26 S(2d) 194 (1946); Wagner v. Milwaukee, 177 Wis 410, 188 NW 487 (1922); CIO v. City of Dallas (Texas), 198 SW(2d) 143 (1946).

goals similar to labor unions would seem to be a finding that such organizations generally seek to force their employee members to do something which is inconsistent with the position of the employee as a government worker. This is not generally true.

This, of course, is a substantial hurdle because the public employee has gained little if he is merely given the right to join organizations, but stopped from bargaining collectively.

The argument in support of the attitude that the public employer should not be required to bargain collectively with public employees can be briefly summarized as follows:

1. The fixing of conditions of work in the public service is a legislative function.
2. Neither the executive nor legislative body may delegate such functions to any outside group.
3. The legislature or executive must be free to change the conditions of employment at any time.[19]

It is submitted that these arguments are based upon a misconception of what is actually meant by good faith collective bargaining, as that phrase has been defined heretofore in this chapter.

§ 6.10 State level—judicial decision or statutory provisions

It is appropriate now to examine the existing status of public employee collective bargaining at the state level.

A number of states, either by judicial decision or by statute, are showing an awareness of the realities of the situation and an understanding of what collective bargaining really means, and are not influenced by the arguments recently summarized as to why collective bargaining on the part of public employees should be treated as illegal.

---

[19] Klaus, "Labor Relations in Public Service," Report of the Committee on State Labor Legislation, Proceedings of Section of Labor Relations Law, American Bar Association, page 147 (1958).

Some states by judicial decision—entirely independent of supporting state statutes—have approved collective bargaining if two conditions exist:

1. The parties enter into it voluntarily.
2. There is no prohibitory state statute.

The leading case exhibiting this philosophy is the 1951 Connecticut Supreme Court decision of *Norwalk Teachers Ass'n.* v. *Board of Education.*[20]

Some jurisdictions[21] have not been content with the possibility that collective bargaining will be initiated through voluntary agreement as sanctioned by judicial decision. These states have passed statutes sanctioning collective bargaining and in many instances have laid down rather specific ground rules.

§ 6.11 Wisconsin's comprehensive statutes

The state of Wisconsin[22] furnishes perhaps the best and most comprehensive example of a statute of such type.

§ 6.12 —Right to negotiate or not negotiate

The statute gives covered employees the right to join labor organizations and to be represented by such organizations in conferences and negotiations with their employers or their representatives on questions of wages, hours and con-

[20] 138 Conn 269, 83 A(2d) 482 (1951). See also: Civil Service Forum v. New York City Transit Authority, 163 NYS(2d) 476, 4 AppDiv(2d) 117 (1957); affd 4 NY(2d) 866, 150 NE(2d) 705, 174 NYS(2d) 234 (1958). Local 266, International Bro. of Elec. Workers v. Salt River Project Agri. Improve. and Power Dist., 78 Ariz 30, 275 P(2d) 393 (1954); Los Angeles Metropolitan Transit Authority v. Brotherhood of R.R. Trainmen, 54 Cal(2d) 684, 355 P(2d) 905 (1960).

[21] AlaskaLaws 1959, ch. 108; MassAnnLaws 40, sec. 46 (1960); Minn StatAnn, sec. 179.52 (Supp. 1960); NHRevStatAnn, sec. 31.13 (1956); IllAnnStat, ch. 127, sec. 63 b 109 (7) (Smith-Hurd Supp. 1960); Fla Stat., sec. 839.22 (1) (1959); RIGenLaw, sec. 36-11-1—36-11-5 (Supp. 1959).

[22] West's WisStatAnn, section 111.70.

ditions of employment. The employees also have the right to refrain from any and all such activities. The statute prohibits municipal employers or employees from interfering with the rights granted by the legislation through discrimination in regard to hire, tenure or other terms or conditions of employment.

§ 6.13 —Wisconsin Employment Relations Board

The Wisconsin Employment Relations Board, which is authorized to administer the statute, has made it clear that any employee organization whose purpose is to represent municipal employees in conferences and negotiations with their employer on questions of wages, hours and conditions of employment, is considered a labor organization, regardless of what name the employees may use to describe their organization. For example, a local teacher association affiliated with the Wisconsin Education Association has been considered a labor organization for the purpose of the statute.

§ 6.14 — —Interpretation of statute

It appeared that the WERB had interpreted the statute as requiring good faith collective bargaining as that term is generally understood in the area of labor relations.[23] In March, 1966, by a two to one vote of the WERB it was announced that the statute did not actually require negotiations because it did not make failure to engage in negotiations an unfair labor practice. The two members of the board that took this position, however, pointed out that if the parties failed to negotiate, the statute provided that the matter be sent to fact finding, as explained hereafter. The dissenting member of the WERB argued that the plain

[23] This has not been challenged in the courts, although there has been some legal argument to the contrary. For a discussion on this point, see Seitz, "Rights of Public School Teachers to Engage in Collective Bargaining and Other Concerted Activities," 1963 Yearbook of School Law (Interstate), at pp. 209-211.

language of the statute indicated to him that it was the intent to require parties to engage in negotiations.[23a]

§ 6.15 — —Representation

Under specific provisions of the statute, the Wisconsin Employment Relations Board passes upon questions of representation and is empowered to enforce the prohibited practice section. Final orders of the board are subject to judicial review.

§ 6.16 — —Elections; separate units

The statute empowers the WERB to hold elections and determine questions of representation. The Act excludes crafts from any unit that the municipal employees may select. The WERB has determined that the term "craft" includes professional employees, such as teachers. Therefore, teachers are assured of being in a separate unit. In respect to a craft the law provides that the board shall not order an election among employees in a craft unit except upon separate petition initiating representation proceedings in such craft unit.

§ 6.17 — —Supervisors as agents of the employer

The board has further determined that supervisors are agents of the municipal employer within the meaning of the statute and, therefore, cannot be included in the same collective bargaining unit with other employees. This determination has been made even though the statute does not specifically exclude supervisory employees from the definition of employees. The reasoning has been that the inclusion of supervisory employees in the same bargaining unit as the employees whom they supervise would conflict with the supervisors' responsibility in performing their management

[23a] The split on the WERB illustrates the need for careful statutory drafting if it is the intent to impose upon the parties the requirement of good faith negotiations, as that term has been delineated in this article.

function and would, therefore, tend to interfere with protected rights of employees to organize and to be represented by organizations of their own choosing. In spite of this attitude, however, the board has held that mere membership of supervisors in a labor organization is not prohibited by the statute. The board has decreed that the ratio of their membership and the question as to whether supervisors hold an office or participate in the formulation of the bargaining policies and progress of the labor organization is the really significant factor in determining whether such labor organization was dominated by the employer.

§ 6.18 —Minority groups of employees

In the industrial and business field exclusive bargaining has become a way of life. Experts from both management and labor concede that it is not practical to expect an employer to bargain with any but the union that represents the majority of the employees in an appropriate unit. In the public employee field, however, the objection has been made that there is something unconstitutional about providing for exclusive bargaining, on the ground that every citizen has a right to petition his government.

Wisconsin has dealt with this matter by providing in section 111.70 (4) (d) that proceedings in representation cases shall be in accordance with Wisconsin statute section 111.05 (1) insofar as applicable. Section 111.05 (1) states that the representatives chosen for the purpose of collective bargaining by the majority of the employees voting in a collective bargaining unit shall be the exclusive representatives of all the employees in such unit for the purpose of collective bargaining, *provided* that any individual employee or minority group of employees in any collective bargaining unit shall have the right at any time to present grievances to their employer in person or through representatives of their own choosing, and the employer shall confer with them in relation thereto. The WERB has interpreted this language to mean that the employer does not have to engage in bargaining with any but the organization that has been certified as the representative of the employees. There have been arguments presented that the statute and the attitude of the board is unconstitutional for the reason indicated above, but to date there has been no judicial litigation or court decision on the matter. The Milwaukee school board and other municipal employers in Wisconsin accept the theory of exclusive bargaining.[23b] It appears to this writer that the proviso in Wisconsin statute section 111.05 (1) answers the objection of those who assert that there is something unconstitutional about providing for exclusive bargaining in the public employee field. By permitting the presentation of grievances by an individual or minority the Wisconsin Act sets up a technique which will enable the employer to learn certain facts which it may want to use when it bargains with the majority, and citizens and minority groups are not denied the right to petition their government.

There has been an additional contention that the wording of Wisconsin statute section 111.70 (4) (d), through its reference to proceedings in representation cases, incorporated only the procedural content of section 111.05 (1) and that the direction in section 111.05 (1) that "representatives chosen for the purpose of collective bargaining by the majority of employees voting in the collective bargaining unit shall be the exclusive representative of all employees in such unit for the purpose of collective bargaining" is the statement of a substantive right. While it is true that section 111.70 (4) (d) refers to proceedings in representation cases being in accordance with the provision of section 111.05 and exclusive recognition may be viewed as the result of an election conducted under section 111.05, it must be noted that

---

[23b] Story, Theory Into Practice, Vol. IV, No. 2, p. 61 (1965). Ohio State University Press.

the statute does not expressly make this distinction between proceedings and result, and if such a basic distinction was intended, it is reasonable to assume that the legislature would have expressed this desire in unequivocal terms. There are other arguments which can be made in favor of sustaining exclusive bargaining. Section 111.70 (4) (d), by its specific language, provides that elections shall be held to determine whether a union shall represent the "employees" of the employer. It does not say that the union shall represent only a majority of the employees of the employer. This language leads to the reasonable conclusion that if a particular labor union wins the allegiance of the majority of the employees within the bargaining unit, it is then entitled to represent all employees in negotiation over wages, hours and working conditions. Furthermore, sections 111.05 (2), (3), (3m) and (4) set forth procedures for the conduct of a secret election to determine whether a majority of the employees desire to be represented by a particular labor organization. If the organization commanding the support of a majority of the employees were permitted to only represent its members in collective bargaining, the elaborate structure of election and the requirement of a secret ballot would seem quite unnecessary.

From the factual standpoint, the indications are that almost all municipal employers clearly desire to bargain on an exclusive basis with the organization that has been selected as the representative of the majority.

Although it appears that the Wisconsin statute pertaining to public employee bargaining is the most comprehensive to date, there is other current legislation. Legislation particularly restricted in operation to teachers was passed in 1965 in Connecticut, Oregon, Washington, and California.

§ 6.19 California statute

The California provision which became effective in September, 1965, is particularly interesting.[23c] The statute was passed for the specific purpose of removing education personnel from the impact of the Government Code which controlled general public employee relations.

The history of the legislation reveals clearly that it does not require good faith bargaining as this article has defined it. It does require a governing board or such administrative officer as it may designate to meet and confer with representatives of employee organizations, upon request, with regard to all matters relating to employment conditions and employer-employee relations, all matters relating to the definition of educational objectives, the determination of the context of courses and curricula, the selection of textbooks and other aspects of the instructional program, to the extent such matters are within the discretion of the board.

The California statute makes clear that it does not adopt the theory of bargaining with an exclusive representative. The Act says that

> in the event there is more than one employee organization representing certified employees, the public school employer . . . shall meet and confer with the representatives of such employee organizations through a negotiating council . . . provided that nothing herein shall prohibit any employee from appearing in his own behalf . . . the negotiating council shall have not more than nine nor less than five members and shall be composed of representatives of those employee organizations who are entitled to representation on the negotiating council. An employee organization representing certified employees shall be entitled to appoint such number of members of the negotiating council as bears as nearly as practicable the same ratio to the total number of members of the negotiating council as the number of

[23c] Amendment to sec. 3501 of Government Code and Addition Art. 5 (commencing with sec. 15080) to ch. 1 of Division 10 of Part 2 of Education Code.

members of the employee organization bears to the total number of certified employees of the public school employer who are members of the employee organizations representing certificated employees.

§ 6.20 Connecticut and Michigan statutes

The Connecticut statute[23d] has some interesting provisions. It expressly recognizes that a bargaining unit may be appropriate which includes supervisory (other than the superintendent) and non-supervisory employees. Or there may be two separate units—one for all employees in positions requiring a teaching or special service certificate, and the other for all employees in positions requiring a supervisory or special service certificate. The legislation provides that when 20 percent of either the teaching or supervisory employees file a petition with the state commissioner of education for separate representation, separate units will be set up. The representative selected is to be the exclusive representative in the unit with a proviso similar to that in Wisconsin as to the right of individual employees to present grievances. The statute sets up a technique for determining the question of representation.

The Michigan Act[23e] applies to all public employees. It authorizes the Michigan Labor Mediation Board to determine the appropriate unit and to conduct a representative election. It requires public employers to negotiate in good faith with the designated exclusive representative on "rates of pay, wages, hours of employment or other conditions of employment."

§ 6.21 Fact finding

In an effort to take care of a bargaining impasse or refusal to negotiate, the Wisconsin statute introduced a pro-

---

[23d] Public Law, sec. 298 (1965).
[23e] Public Law, sec. 379 (1965).

vision for fact finding.[23f] If an employer or a union fails or refuses to meet or negotiate in good faith at reasonable times in a bona fide effort to arrive at settlement or if after a reasonable period of negotiations the parties are deadlocked, the WERB is empowered to appoint a fact finder when it is satisfied that a deadlock exists. The fact finder is authorized to hold hearings and must make written findings and recommendations which are to be made public. The fact finder has no power to enforce his recommendations. The hope is that the promulgation of recommendations will enlist the support of public opinion in finding a solution. The cost of fact finding is to be shared by the parties.

The WERB is directed not to initiate fact-finding proceedings in any case when the municipal employer, through ordinance or otherwise, has established fact-finding techniques substantially in compliance with the statute.

§ 6.22 Settlement reduced to writing

Collective bargaining has as an end product the objective of an employer-employee contract. The federal law recognizes this. The Wisconsin statute specifically states that upon the completion of negotiations with an employee organization representing a majority of the employees in a collective unit, if a settlement is reached, the employer shall reduce the same to writing, either in the form of an ordinance, resolution or agreement. It is stated that the term for which a contract shall remain in effect shall not exceed one year.

§ 6.23 Statutory advantages

The existence of a statute in the field of public employee bargaining is of major significance. As has been indicated, courts may sanction voluntary bargaining in the absence of statute, but this will not always insure the desired result.

[23f] Some of the other statutes also have provision for fact finding after impasse. No statute makes the decision of a fact finder binding.

For instance, a statute can spell out election procedure to be used in the determination of a majority representative in an appropriate unit. It can make clear that bargaining is to be on an exclusive basis with the organization that represents the majority of the employees in an appropriate unit. It can express other intents. If there is no statute, whatever attempts are made at bargaining may break down in arguments over procedure and over such questions as exclusive representation.

Since the Wisconsin statute was used as an example, it perhaps should be said that the statute does present some language which has resulted in arguments as to the intent of meaning. There will undoubtedly be amendments by way of clarifications and additions. In the field of public employee bargaining—still somewhat of an experimental area —it may in some jurisdictions be difficult to pass a statute which is a model of clarity. Most statutory efforts, however, will produce a better result than to depend upon voluntary arrangement, if the community feels that employee relations will be fostered by stimulating collective bargaining.

In connection with statutory provisions it should be noted, as indicated previously, that Washington, California, Connecticut and several other states have manifested an interest in keeping the administration of teacher bargaining out of the hands of the state industrial or employment relations board and have made provisions for a separate professional board.

In some statutes,[24] including those of Wisconsin, there is a provision aimed at assisting in connection with negotiations between the public employer and employees. It is the provision for mediation, when such help is requested by

---

[24] AlaskaLaws 1959, ch. 108; FlaStat, sec. 839.22 (1) (1959); Ill StatAnn, ch. 127, sec. 63 b 109 (7) (Smith-Hurd Supp. 1960); MassAnn Laws, ch. 40, sec. 4 c (1960); MichCompLaws, secs. 423.201 to 423.208 (1948); MinnStatAnn, sec. 179.52 (Supp. 1960); NHRevStatAnn, sec. 31.3 (1955); NDLaws, ch. 219 (1951); OreRevStat, sec. 662 (1953); RIGen Law, secs. 36-11-1 to 36-11-5 (Supp. 1959); WisLaws 1959, sec. 111.70.

both parties. In Wisconsin when such request is made, the Wisconsin Employment Relations Board may function.

§ 6.24 Other problems

There are a number of additional matters that merit discussion if public employee bargaining is approved in a particular jurisdiction, either by judicial decision or through legislation.

§ 6.25 —Union security agreement

One is the question of whether a public employer can enter into a union security agreement with a majority union, requiring that all employees in an appropriate unit must, within a set period of time after employment (commonly thirty days), join the union which is recognized as representing the employees in the appropriate unit. Unless outlawed by right-to-work laws, this term can be incorporated and enforced in labor contracts in industry. To date there has been no decision which has sanctioned such a provision in the public employer-employee area. Indeed, a 1959 Montana case[25] has come out forcibly against the validity of the union security clause.

Two other questions are whether a negotiated contract could provide for the agency shop, or for the check off of dues.

§ 6.26 —Agency shop; check off of dues

The agency shop is designed to meet the argument that no individual should be compelled to join a union (and become subject to its discipline) against his will as a condition of getting or keeping a job, and the counter-argument for eliminating the "free rider," i.e., an employee who is willing to accept the benefits of collective bargaining without paying his fair share of the cost of the bargaining proc-

[25] Benson v. School Dist. No. 1, 136 Mont 77, 344 P(2d) 117 (1959).

ess.[26] The opponents of the agency shop contend that it is unfair to require an employee who is unwilling to join a union to pay money into its treasury.

It would appear that if the legislature of a state so decreed, language looking toward the permission to include a union shop clause or check off of dues provision in a contract would be found lawful in some jurisdictions. If the legislature did wish to grant such permission, it would undoubtedly require more than a simple majority vote of the employees. Politically it might be quite difficult to induce a legislature to sanction a union or an agency shop clause in a contract involving public employees.[26a] Certainly if the legislature were disposed to act, it should put up a barrier against money paid in by nonunion men being used for political or other purposes not germane to the collective bargaining process.

Even if legislatures did make union shop and agency shop permissive clauses in contracts in the public employee field, it seems reasonable to predict that many state courts would find the provisions improper. It would be quite likely that such courts would find applicable the basic philosophy that the Montana Supreme Court[27] expressed, in dealing with the problem of insertion of a union security clause into a contract when no statute existed. The court concluded that agreements by the board to hire only union members would be illegal discrimination.

§ 6.27 —Arbitration

Another significant question is whether a negotiated contract can provide for binding arbitration of grievances

[26] For a review of the problem see the late Senator Taft's comments in Senate Labor Committee Report, 80th Congress, First Session, Report No. 105, April 17, 1947.

[26a] In October 1965 the Wisconsin legislature did sanction an agency shop contract in the field of municipal public employment. Teachers, however, were excepted from the impact of the statute. The governor vetoed the act.

[27] Supra, note 25.

arising under a contract. Many attacks on this kind of provision manifest a failure to discern that the proposal is limited to the arbitration of grievances arising under a contract. The assumption that induces many to object appears to be that an arbitration proposal involves calling in an outsider to write a term into a contract, if the parties cannot agree. No one is presently seriously making such proposal.

Numerous courts, however, have given consideration to the matter of arbitration of grievances under a contract. Those who oppose the clause as invalid reason that it constitutes a complete abdication of school board authority. The Ohio[28] Common Pleas court, for example, has indicated that it would be a vain and futile thing for a board to refer issues to an arbitrator who, with the best intentions, might make an award which, because of conflicting statutes, would be legally impossible for the board to accept.

This is essentially the same argument outlined in this chapter in connection with some objections that have been made to collective bargaining. In facing up to the argument, it was pointed out that it is always necessary in the field of public employee bargaining to be aware of the problem of colliding with statutes. So, too, in the arbitration area it is obvious that an arbitrator could not render a binding decision which would collide with some existing statutes. Some statutes would, indeed, stand as a barrier against referring matters to an arbitrator. For example, if a tenure statute specifically sets up the procedure in respect to discharge for cause, the statute must be followed, and the matter cannot simply be referred to an arbitrator.

A recently signed contract between a union and the city of Milwaukee, Wisconsin, furnishes an illustration of what can be done by way of providing for arbitration in a labor agreement when the allegation is in direct conflict with a

[28] City of Cleveland v. Division 268, Amalgamated Assn. of Street, Elec. R. and Motor Coach Employees of Amer., 30 OhioOp 395 (1945).

statutory hurdle.[29] In Milwaukee the law imposes responsibility on the Civil Service Commission to decide disciplinary disputes. The labor contract, therefore, makes provision that such disputes will be referred to an arbitrator for an advisory opinion. This opinion will be sent to the Civil Service Commission for ultimate decision. Under the contract the Civil Service Commission is still allowed sole authority to arbitrate grievances on promotion and job evaluation. Disputes on seniority rights, work rules and the application of the contract's terms on wages, hours and working conditions are to be referred to binding arbitration. The arbitrator is to be selected from a panel supplied by the Wisconsin Employment Relations Board.

The New York City Board of Education agreement with its teachers—perhaps the most comprehensive teacher contract that has been negotiated to date—shows a voluntary effort to incorporate the kind of arbitration clause that is legal. Under the New York contract the recourse to an arbitrator is available only for grievances involving the application or interpretation of the agreement. The arbitrator is specifically prohibited from making any decision which is contrary to or inconsistent with the terms of the agreement, or which involves the exercise of discretion by the board or limits or interferes in any way with the powers, duties and responsibilities of the board under law. It is quite obvious that the arbitrator is not put in a position to write in contractual terms.

The *Norwalk* case exhibits judicial approval of an arbitration clause.[30]

A recent decision of an arbitrator under the New York

---

[29] Although the Wisconsin statute makes no provision for introducing an arbitration clause into any agreement that may be reached, the legality of such provision is supported by City of Madison v. Frank Lloyd Wright Foundation, 20 Wis(2d) 361, 122 NW(2d) 409 (1963).

[30] Norwalk Teachers Assn. v. Board of Ed., 138 Conn 269, 83 A(2d) 482 (1951).

City contract reveals one individual example as to just how narrow the arbitration power can be regarded.[30a]

Under the grievance procedure provided in the New York contract the superintendent of schools (in Step 3) ruled that a teacher, by reason of terms in the contract, was entitled to a duty-free lunch period "at the earliest possible date." The teacher brought the matter to arbitration, on the ground that the superintendent's decision did not provide him and "other employees similarly situated" with compensatory time off equivalent to the amount of duty-free lunch time that they failed to receive during approximately 36 weeks of the 1963-64 school year.

Both parties requested the arbitrator to limit his decision in the first instance to the arbitrability of the narrow issue presented by the teacher—that is, the right to compensatory time off.

The decision was that the question as presented was not arbitrable.

The reasoning of the arbitrator was as follows: The history of negotiations showed that the independent opinion of an arbitrator was to be sought only as to the meaning of the agreement's substantive provisions regarding working conditions. (In other words it did not envision award of a remedy which would cost money.)

It was felt that the arbitrator could not make an award which would cost money because the Education Law in New York clearly showed that the board could not delegate its responsibility for use of available funds. The arbitrator also commented that the Education Law dictated that the board could not delegate its authority as regards extent of needed instruction.

The decision stated that an arbitrator cannot intrude upon important areas of the board's "discretion" and "policy making" function as set forth in Education Law. If the legis-

---

[30a] Board of Education of the City of New York and United Federation of Teachers, 44 LA 929 (1965).

lature had intended to make it possible for the arbitrator to substitute his judgment in such areas, it could have and would have made such intent clear, the arbitrator reasoned.

The arbitrator talked about compensatory time off adding up to as much as $7,000,000 to $8,000,000, or a school closing of approximately 12 days. It is surely obvious that this had an effect on the arbitrator, although he states that potential liability makes no difference. He said that even if it were $10 "the basic conclusion must be and is that the board cannot delegate to the arbitrator its responsibility for determining how to allocate its funds."

This attitude, it needs be repeated, is because of the way the arbitrator read the New York Education Law, sections 2554 (9), 2576 (5) and 2576 (7).

The arbitrator took occasion to warn that even if the Education Law did not stand in the way of the arbitrator, a contract would have to be very clear as to intent before the arbitrator could disburse funds by way of remedy.

After concluding as he did, the arbitrator undertook to set forth some observations. He felt that there was still merit in the arbitration provisions in the New York City contract. He said:

> in the present situation the union has been able to achieve significant gains in connection with the resolution of grievances, in that under Article VI (which deals with grievance procedure and arbitration) of the contract the board has committed itself to arbitration of a broad range of substantive issues that may arise concerning working conditions, especially since supervisors are understandably reluctant to be brought to the attention of those in authority above them on charges of unfairness to teachers under them. . . .
>
> A large complex educational system inevitably lends itself to situations where there may be an abuse of power by those in supervisory positions. The recognition of this possibility by the board and the union, with their

> resultant agreement on the beneficial provisions of Article VI, is an important step forward in the area of improving working conditions, and undoubtedly has an influence on those in direct authority, with recognition by them of the contractual rights, as well as the dignity and respect due a person who, as a result of years of preparation, has attained professional status.

In view of such observation it should be remembered that in the arbitration matter just discussed in Step 3 of the grievance, the teacher received a ruling that she was to be given duty-free lunch periods "at the earliest possible date." It was not too long after such decision that additional personnel were assigned to the school, and duty-free lunch periods were provided.

All that the arbitrator concluded was that he had no jurisdiction to award compensatory time off to make whole for free time lost in the past.

§ 6.28 Right to strike, sanctions, and corrective measures

No discussion concerning the right of teachers to engage in collective bargaining ought to terminate without some mention of the legality of public employee use of certain concerted activities intended to exert pressure on school boards, with the objective of attaining certain contract goals.

The activity that suggests itself for analysis, in the first instance, is the right to strike. In the field of industrial relations the right is largely preserved by statutes and courts. In the field of government the right has been found not to exist. To date the judicial attitude in this respect is uniform. All courts and authorities[31] agree that the right does not exist. The philosophy which supports the conclusion has

---

[31] For a summary of authorities, see Seasongood and Barry, "Unionization of Public Employees," 21 UCinLRev 327 (1952). Also see Ryne, Labor Unions and Municipal Employee Law.

been variously expressed. The Attorney General of Minnesota told the Board of Regents of the University of Minnesota that "should we accept the doctrine permitting strikes, we would in effect transfer to such employees all legislative, executive and judicial powers now vested in the duly elected public officers." Woodrow Wilson called strikes by public employees "an interminable crime against civilization."[32] The *Norwalk*[33] case quotes Franklin D. Roosevelt, whom it identifies as certainly no enemy of labor, as saying, "A strike of public employees manifests nothing less than an intent on their part to prevent or obstruct the operation of government, and such action is unthinkable and interminable." *Norwalk* goes on to say,

> Under our system, the government is established by and run for all the people, not for the benefit of any person or group. The profit motive is absent. It should be the aim of every employee of the government to do his or her part to make it function as efficiently and economically as possible. The drastic remedy of the organized strike to enforce the demands of a union of government employees is in direct contravention of this principle.

As far as striking against school boards is concerned, there is an additional good argument. Teachers cannot forget that they work in a delicate area where it is of the utmost importance that young people be encouraged to respect the legitimate authority of school personnel. It is submitted that teachers risk such respect when they go on strike. Even granted that sometimes teachers may have a very good cause, it appears that immature young people in school may not be able to appreciate the fact, and may very likely feel that authority has been flaunted. Certainly it seems very disconcerting when teachers and teachers' unions openly

[32] These attitudes are quoted by Vogel in "What About the Right of the Public Employee," 1 LaborLJ 604 (1950).

[33] Supra, note 30.

defy existing law and assert that regardless of the law, they will strike.

It would seem that teacher picketing of the schools may have very much the same effect on young minds as the strike effort. Although the courts have continued to recognize that there is much free speech in picketing, they have also clearly acknowledged that picketing contains elements other than free speech. It may very well be, therefore, that a state, by statute, may adopt a policy against picketing of schools by teachers. If such policy is enunciated, courts could very well sustain the statute.

Those who argue that teachers should have a right to strike assert basically that without the right, teachers have no realistic way of advancing their cause against an adamant school board. They further contend that the general language condemning strikes on the part of public employees should not be applied to all employees, but that the decision should be realistically grounded on the emergency created. Those who make this argument would grant that police and firemen should have no right to strike but they would, for example, not give the same support to a law forbidding street maintenance employees from striking. Even on the assumption that there might be some merit in such distinctions, it is by no means clear that courts would or should conclude that teachers have the right to strike. It does not seem unrealistic to recognize extreme interference with public welfare when the education of a child is affected by the absence of teachers from the class room.

The fact finding process provided in the Wisconsin statute previously described is designed to give public employees help in lieu of the right to strike. It must be remembered, however, that the fact finder under the Wisconsin statute has no power to enforce his decision. Fact finding is grounded upon the hope that the sympathy of public opinion will be enlisted behind a fact finding conclusion.

It will be necessary to wait for experience under the Wisconsin statute and others that provide for fact finding to determine if public opinion will so respond when a response to a fact finding holding may require an increase in taxes. The answer will not always appear as a result of action taken immediately after a fact finding decision has been rendered. Current budget problems may force postponement of implementation of a fact finding decision. Ultimately, however, information can be gathered on the efficacy of fact finding decisions.

If it should be finally discovered that fact finding is not in reality influencing public opinion and in turn inducing a change in the position of the public employer or a union, the fact finding is really not much of a substitute for the right to strike. If this is found to be the result, the writer suggests the possibility of further experimentation with the fact finding process. If fact finding is not successful at the local level, provision could be made for the decision to be reviewed by an impartial out-of-state fact finding board made up of a leading professional educator, a civic leader and an impartial chairman. Provision could be made to permit teacher strikes if this fact finding body on review supported the initial findings and the board remained adamant. If this happened, it would appear that school personnel ought to be able to convince pupils and the general public that such a strike does not flaunt legitimate law and authority.

There presently remains the question as to whether, other than fact finding, there is any effective pressure that teachers can use in place of the strike. The National Education Association has proposed sanctions. Under this suggestion teacher organizations encourage teachers not to return a signed contract, and advise teachers not to accept jobs in the area. It is true that, if effective, sanctions have the same result as a strike, in the sense that teachers are not in the classrooms. The great difference, however, is that teachers are not leaving their posts during a contract term.

It is hard to find any illegality in the sanction, which is sparked only by an appeal to teachers not to sign contracts or take jobs in an area. This sort of appeal is surely free speech and the individual certainly has a constitutional right to determine if he will work. Illegality would appear only if the organization induced some kind of boycott pressure which resulted in loss of job opportunities to teachers who did not heed the call to sanction.

In spite of the fact that strikes by public employees and teachers are held to be illegal, they have occurred and are likely to take place again. From a purely practical viewpoint, teachers en masse cannot be discharged even though their conduct is treated as illegal. Perhaps the most effective way to attack the strike problem is to aim legislation at the union treasury if the union calls the strike. Another approach is to pass legislation similar to the Condon-Wadlin law in New York.[34] Under the most recent 1963 amendments to the New York Act, provision was made for penalties against those who strike, in the form of no salary increases for six months, probation with loss of tenure for one year and salary deduction to twice the daily compensation. Prior to the time the amendments were passed, harsher penalties in the New York law were not enforced. The amended Act was to remain in effect until July, 1965. Any tax payer could initiate the action. The amendments have expired and the law has reverted to the harsher Condon-Wadlin penalties.

A complete analysis of experience under the Condon-Wadlin Act is presented in a recent issue of ILR Research,[35] published by the New York State School of Industrial and Labor Relations of Cornell University, New York. The author concludes that the Act has been used upstate to stop strikes, but asserts this is probably because of

---

34 See Pruzan v. Board of Education, 209 NYS(2d) 966 (1960) for a court discussion involving the constitutionality of the Act.

35 Rosenzweig, "The Condon-Wadlin Act Re-examined," ILR Research, Vol. XI, No. 1, pp. 3-8 (1965).

the lack of politically powerful employee organizations in the areas. The facts, it is stated, indicate that the Act has never been fully invoked against a large group when that group was a strong union.

Since the amendments to Condon-Wadlin, adopted on April 23, 1963, there have been four strikes of public employees in New York City.

On January 31, 1965, the longest strike of public employees in New York City's history was ended. After twenty-eight days the striking welfare workers, members of the union, voted to accept the recommendation of a citizens' committee appointed by Mayor Wagner. The major stumbling block to settlement of the strike had been the Condon-Wadlin Act, and the committee recommended that the city delay imposing penalties under the Act until their constitutionality could be tested by the unions.

In July, 1964, the Act was invoked in New York City against a one-day wildcat strike of 648 ferry workers, members of National Maritime Union. The workers did sign waivers of three days' pay: one day for their absence from work and two days as a penalty under Condon-Wadlin. But, in spite of the fact that the Act provided that strikers were not to receive pay increases for six months, the workers got an immediate increase, won by the union, of fifty cents an hour over a three-year period.

In August, 1964, the New York City day camp teachers, members of UFT, staged a "mass resignation" for six days. They won salary increases and other benefits. It is not clear whether the Condon-Wadlin Act was actually invoked. The superintendent of schools stated, "Since settlement has been reached, I am sure that the Board of Education will want to exercise every bit of leniency within the provisions of the law."

After analyzing the Condon-Wadlin experience, the writer in ILR Research recommends repeal of the Act and passage of the bill proposed in the 1962 Staff Report to the New

York Joint Legislative Committee on Industrial and Labor Conditions. Among the recommendations are:

(1) Greater flexibility in penalties, by replacing the Condon-Wadlin penalties with those for misconduct as contained in the state Civil Service law, permitting choice between reprimand, fine of not more than $100, suspension without pay for not more than two months, demotion, or dismissal.

(2) Addition of requirement that the state attorney general seek an injunction immediately when the law has been violated.

And most fundamental of all, the suggestion is made that the law guarantee the right of public workers to join or enter employee organizations, that there be provisions for collective dealing and grievance processing, so that some of the causes of strikes will be eliminated and that, further, there be provisions for mediation and binding arbitration of disputes arising under the collective agreement.

Another effective way of dealing with strikes is through clauses negotiated in the labor agreement. The contract could provide that a strike called by the union would entitle the employer to recover specific named damages. The contract could further provide that employees taking part in an unauthorized strike would be subject to discharge or loss of pay and certain benefits. In the case of such a strike, the union could be obligated to immediately order strikers back to work.

§ 6.29 Looking toward the future

It seems appropriate by way of conclusion to make some comments looking toward the future. In this respect it is logical to return directly to thinking about the issue of public employee bargaining versus school board authority. This chapter has had the intent of establishing that school board authority will not be undermined just because collective bargaining is decreed by law. It is submitted that the tide is running in favor of giving public employees more bargaining rights. It does not appear that the trend can be stopped for long by school boards. It seems that boards will have no more success in this respect than the industrial employers of the 1930's who, as has been previously commented upon, tried to halt the movement to give the laborer increased bargaining rights with very much the same kind of arguments that some boards of education are using today. The principal contention was that of improper delegation of authority.

It is submitted that boards of education might very well stop trying to label provisions for collective bargaining illegal and turn their attention toward working out procedures which will make of public employee bargaining something which is practical and expeditious. There definitely are problems in the procedural area. Budget dates, for example, suggest setting up an intelligent time table for bargaining. Boards will undoubtedly want to give consideration to the question of who should represent them at the bargaining table. The board will want to face up to whether it might be unwise to have the superintendent the constant negotiator. Some limitations on size of the bargaining teams may be in order. If provisions are to be made for fact finding, the matter of consideration of time tables becomes even more necessary.

It is particularly important to consider the role of the superintendent of schools. He holds the position of executive officer of the board and is also charged with providing professional leadership and administrative direction to the teaching staff. He cannot avoid playing a key role in negotiations, but it does seem unwise to have the superintendent personally participate at the bargaining table or elsewhere in the actual mechanics of bargaining. Because of his intimate knowledge of all aspects of administration, including budget making, he can give realistic guidance to the bargaining committee; he should however, not be cast in any role which would deter employees from candidly seeking his advice.

The composition of a bargaining committee seems all-important. Many school administrators assert that a board of education should not be larger than 5 to 7 members. It has been further suggested by some school administrators that if the board is of such size, the entire body should sit at the bargaining table. This may work in communities that are not too large and where the issues are not complex. It seems that in larger communities, where problems tend to become more complex, the entire board will not be able to contribute time to attend all bargaining sessions. Then, too, some boards are larger than 5 to 7 members. Certainly, bargaining tends to become too unwieldy if a large board sits constantly during negotiations. If it is not feasible as to time or size for the entire board to sit throughout all bargaining sessions, it will be necessary to work out some kind of bargaining committee arrangement whereby membership may shift from time to time. The committee should seek the services of a negotiator skilled in collective bargaining, and could very well include a lawyer experienced in the area of employee relations.

Discussions by some educators seem to indicate that there will be no need for such specialists because, unless bargaining is to take on the nature of "horse trading," the board and the employees should honestly exchange facts and arrive at decisions in very short order. It is true that bargaining should not be "horse trading." Even though it is not, it does, however, take time and expertise of high order to resolve issues and positions honestly assumed by both sides of the bargaining table. The experience of those who have actually participated in negotiating sessions induces this realistic conclusion. The bargaining committees on both sides should have the benefit of advice of specialists in substantive areas under consideration.

Most importantly, there is a need at all times for realistic communication between any negotiating committee (if the full board does not sit) and the board of education.

A problem requiring the most careful thinking is the procedure relative to open bargaining sessions. It is unrealistic to carry on collective bargaining entirely through open meetings. On the other hand, in the public employee field the people have a significant right to know the facts and issues discussed. At appropriate intervals the public must be given the position of the parties.

Many states have statutes requiring open meetings of governmental bodies. Wisconsin is illustrative.[35a] The Wisconsin Act provides that no formal action of any kind shall be introduced, deliberated upon or adopted at any closed executive session or closed meeting of any state and local governing and administrative bodies. Certain exceptions are set forth. A 1965[35b] opinion of the Wisconsin attorney general finds the exception broad enough to cover the negotiations of a municipality and a labor organization. However, it is made clear that the formal introduction, deliberation and adoption of the bargaining recommendations by the elected body must be at open meetings.

For reasons indicated in the body of this article, it seems expeditious to guide collective bargaining through specific statutory provisions. Collective bargaining is not an evil. There are, of course, legitimate pressures in collective bargaining. Although the pressure does not require capitulation, it is intended to create an atmosphere which will insure a give and take in the form of responses to demands, and will often result in counterproposals and full explanations when demands are rejected. This process is calculated to produce some sane and logical compromises. By a suc-

[35a] West's Wisconsin Statutes Annotated, sec. 14.90.

[35b] August 19.

cession of free choices each party determines the order of importance of his bargaining proposals. As these proposals are presented, each party balances what is desired against known costs of unresolved disagreement. These costs, on the one side, may be such things as loss of competent employees and the fostering of a general low morale, and on the other side the loss of community support if unreasonable demands are made.

Finally, it seems important to draw to the attention of those school boards that feel that collective bargaining means capitulation, the philosophy expressed by the United States Supreme Court in a December, 1964 decision.[36] The Court clearly revealed that collective bargaining does not connote capitulation and that it has a very important function. The Court pointedly commented that although it is not possible to say whether a satisfactory solution can be reached, the national labor policy is founded upon a determination that the chances are good enough to warrant subjecting issues to the process of collective bargaining.

If boards of education will engage in good faith collective bargaining and work out satisfactory procedures, there is every reason to believe that there will be created a situation which will ultimately result in a climate that will produce better education for children.

---

[36] Fibreboard Paper Products Corp. v. NLRB, 379 US 203, 85 SCt 398 (1964).

Epilog

YESTERDAY IS THE PROLOGUE

The operation of the local school district by the legal agent of the state, the school board, can be dynamic, regressive, or passive. The legal problems placed before the school board change somewhat in content but over the years the state and federal courts have acted rather similarly in upholding basic principles. On the state level, the courts have been very consistent in stating that the local school board can do those things which the state mandates, permits, or directs it to do within the state constitutional provisions. Within these limitations, the school board has discretionary power that may not be capricious or arbitrary. On the federal level, the most notable change has been in decisions involving the segregation issue. But even on the federal level the courts have upheld the general powers of the school board.

The general emphasis in this book has been to show the importance for the proper organization of the school board to carry out its tasks. At times, the school board has failed to recognize that it is the agent of the state. Recently, at the 1966 state convention of an association of school boards, the audience, made up of school board members, booed when the executive secretary of the association made reference to the simple fact that the local school board was acting as an agent of the state. If there is misunderstanding on this fundamental fact, there is likely to be more misunderstanding on issues facing any school board.

The school board must meet all statutory requirements for holding and conducting meetings, keeping proper minutes and records, and conduct itself in the best interests for public education. The school board and individual board members are subject to remedies against them. The school board cannot delegate its powers to other agents or agencies, but may delegate its ministerial duties.

The carrying out of the ministerial duties of the school board are usually delegated to the chief administrator and other employees of the school district. The relationship of the chief administrator and the staff with the school board seems to have become more complex in our changing society. With the advent of larger school districts and all of the administrative problems connected with largeness, the emphasis on sound school board organization cannot be underestimated. Although a school board may be legally organized, the need for communications seems to be paramount. If the school board is to retain a dynamic interest in the variety of school problems, it seems necessary to establish communication procedures. How can the school board keep in close touch with the citizenry without violating administrative relationships with the administration staff? How can the citizenry communicate with the school board? One of the major charges today is that the citizenry cannot reach the school board regarding issues and problems. Does the establishment of a bureaucratic administration hamper communications and lead to misunderstanding? The emphasis should be on the understanding of the issues in the existing problems. It is also mandatory that the school board, the professional staff, the nonprofessional staff, and the citizens understand the legal structure under which all must operate. If the legal structure needs to be changed, it must be understood that, in general, such change must be initiated on the state level.

Probably in no two areas have we witnessed such need for sound communication procedures as in the problems of de facto segregation and collective negotiations—two current problems of school boards. The word communication has a connotation and a detonation that mandates a willingness to understand rather than just listen. Communication is not unilateral but bilateral or multilateral.

Current issues in collective negotiations being reported throughout the United States illustrate the general lack of understanding of the issues involved. Recently in a state which has statutory collective negotiations provisions, the nonprofessional staff entered negotiations through its labor union representative and requested the inclusion of a number of days for sick leave. The school board was shocked because the request was a drastic reduction in the days of sick leave permitted under existing school board policy. An analysis of the situation seems to indicate that the emphasis was to establish power. In another community in another state, negotiations have come to an impasse because the school board and the professional staff seem unable or unwilling to communicate with each other. The professional staff cannot or does not want to appraise the financial problems of the school district. In turn, the school board wishes to remove the salary index in the salary schedule because of its effect on the total financial picture, in spite of the general agreement by professional organizations that a salary index is a sound basis for a salary schedule.

School boards will be faced with the implementation of new legislation. Currently, states are passing new laws regarding segregation. It may be predicted that more litigation will take place to test the constitutionality of the laws passed. The more active front seems to be in the area of collective negotiations. The trend seems to be for more states to establish statutory provisions for collective negotiations for public employees. In this area, it may be predicted that some litigation will take place regarding the powers of quasi-judicial boards which have, in general, been given powers under the statutes to implement the intent of the legislature. Currently, in the state of Wisconsin, a lower court has held that the Wisconsin Employment Relations Board exceeded its power when it mandated a school board to reinstate a teacher previously dismissed.[1] This case has been appealed by the Wisconsin Employment Relations Board and the decision by the Wisconsin Supreme Court will be most important.

What will be the legal problems in the future ? Yesterday is the prologue.

---

[1] Muskego-Norway Consolidated Schools, Joint School Dist. No. 9, Town of Muskego, Waukesha County, and Town of Norway, Racine County; Robert J. Kreuser, Jack G. Refling, Paul Ussel and Charles Ladd v. Wisconsin Employment Relations Board, Circuit Court Branch 2, Waukesha County, Wisconsin, March 1, 1966.

TABLE OF CASES

References are to section numbers

Miami Water Works, Local No. 654 v. Miami, 157 Fla 445, 26 S(2d) 194 (1946), 6.9

Moore v. Babb (Ky), 343 SW(2d) 373 (1960), 3.3

Mugford v. Mayor and City Council of Baltimore, 185 Md 206, 44 A(2d) 745 (1945), 6.9, 6.27

NLRB v. American Aggregate Co., 335 F(2d) 253 (5th Cir., 1964), 6.4

NLRB v. American Nat. Ins. Co., 343 US 395, 96 LEd 1027, 72 SCt 824 (1952), 6.4

NLRB v. Katz, 369 US 736, 8 LEd(2d) 230, 82 SCt 1107 (1962), 6.6

NLRB v. Insurance Agents Internat. Union, AFL-CIO, 361 US 477, 4 LEd(2d) 454, 80 SCt 419 (1960), 6.3

NLRB v. Item Co., 220 F(2d) 956 (5th Cir., 1955), 6.6

NLRB v. Montgomery Ward & Co., 133 F(2d) 676 (9th Cir., 1943), 6.3

NLRB v. Pilling & Sons Co., 119 F(2d) 32 (3d Cir., 1941), 6.3

NLRB v. Truitt Mfg. Co., 351 US 149, 100 LEd 1027, 76 SCt 753 (1956), 6.6

NLRB v. Wooster Division of Borg-Warner Corp., 356 US 342, 2 LEd(2d) 823, 78 SCt 718 (1958), 6.5

Neal v. Bryant (Fla), 149 S(2d) 529 (1962), 1.9

New York Post Corp. v. Moses, 210 NYS(2d) 88, 12 AppDiv(2d) 243 (1961), 4.9

Norwalk Teachers Assn. v. Board of Ed., 138 Conn 269, 83 A(2d) 482 (1951), 6.10, 6.27

Noxubee Co. v. Long, 141 Miss 72, 106 So 83 (1925), 2.5

Nutter v. Santa Monica, 74 CalApp(2d) 292, 168 P(2d) 741 (1946), 6.9

People ex rel. Fursman v. Chicago, 278 Ill 318, 116 NE 158 (1917), 6.8

People ex rel. Gibson v. Peller, 34 IllApp(2d) 372, 181 NE(2d) 376 (1962), 2.7

People ex rel. Stewart v. Chicago, M. and St. P. R. Co., 326 Ill 179, 157 NE 200 (1927), 2.4

Perez v. Board of Police Comm'rs., 78 CalApp(2d) 638, 178 P(2d) 537 (1947), 6.8

Phillip, State ex rel. v. Public School Retirement System, 364 Mo 395, 262 SW(2d) 569 (en banc, 1953), 3.4

Powers v. Spinner (Mass), 202 NE(2d) 246 (1964), 3.3

Pruzan v. Board of Ed., 209 NYS(2d) 966 (1960), 6.28

Quisenberry v. School Dist., 75 Neb 47, 105 NW 982 (1905), 2.5

Tate v. School Dist., 324 Mo 477, 23 SW(2d) 1013, 70 ALR 771 (1929), 2.2

Tavener v. Elk Rapids, Ind., School Dist., 341 Mich 244, 67 NW(2d) 136 (1954), 2.5

Taylor v. Board of Ed. (NY), 191 FSupp 181 (1961), appeal dismissed 288 F(2d) 600, 195 FSupp 231, aff'd 294 F(2d) 36, stay denied 82 SCt 10, cert. den. 82 SCt 382, 3.6, 5.5

United States v. Cruikshank, 92 US 542 (1876), 4.2

Virginia, Ex parte, 100 US 339 (1880), 5.4

Van Allen v. McCleary, 211 NYS(2d) 501 (1961), 3.4

Wagner v. Milwaukee, 177 Wis 410, 188 NW 487 (1922), 6.9

Wagner v. Redmond (La), 127 S(2d) 275 (1960), 3.4

Walters' Appeal, In re, 270 Wis 561, 72 NW(2d) 535 (1955), 3.5, 3.6

Webb v. Board of Ed. (Ill), 223 FSupp 466 (1963), 5.5

White v. NLRB, 255 F(2d) 564 (5th Cir., 1958), 6.4

INDEX

References are to sections unless otherwise indicated